Truly Wonderful
Puddings&Desserts

Truly Wonderful
Puddings&Desserts

Susan Brookes

Photography by Michelle Garrett

HAMLYN

To Richard and Judy, with love and thanks

Acknowledgements

Art Director: Jacqui Small

Executive Art Editor: Penny Stock

Designer: Louise Leffler

Executive Editor: Susan Haynes

Editor: Kathy Steer

Production Controller: Melanie Frantz

Photography and Styling: Michelle Garrett

Home Economist: Bridget Sargeson

Notes

Both metric and imperial measurements have been given in all recipes.

Use one set of measurements only and not a mixture of both.

Standard level spoon measurements are used in all recipes.

1 tablespoon = one 15 ml spoon

1 teaspoon = one 5 ml spoon

Eggs should be size 3 unless otherwise stated. Some recipes contain raw
eggs. Readers are reminded of the advice from the Department of
Health that it would be prudent for readers, particularly those who
are more vulnerable, such as pregnant women, invalids, the elderly,
babies and young children, to avoid eating uncooked eggs.
Milk should be full fat unless otherwise stated.

First published in Great Britain in 1995 by Hamlyn

an imprint of Reed Consumer Books Limited

Michelin House, 81 Fulham Road, London SW3 6RB

and Auckland, Melbourne, Singapore and Toronto

Text copyright © 1995 Susan Brookes

Design copyright © 1995 Reed International Books Limited

ISBN 0 600 58 716 9

A CIP catalogue record for this book is available from the British Library.

Produced by Mandarin Offset
Printed and bound in Hong Kong

Contents

Introduction

The British are famous for their puddings. In fact, puddings were in the vanguard of the renaissance in our cooking. One of the early signs of the revival was the formation of pudding clubs in many places across the country, where enthusiasm made a mere curtsey in the direction of a savoury starter before getting down to the serious business of the evening – sampling six or eight or even ten delicious puddings, discoursing learnedly on the merits of each and even sending for second helpings to be sure a judgement was fair.

The enthusiasm of these aficionados soon spread. Restaurants saw a resurgence in requests for rice pudding, bread and butter pudding and jam roly poly, alongside a range of desserts that grew daily more diverse. That range is, I hope, reflected in the breadth of variety offered by the recipes in this book. Everyone should find something to suit, from fruit desserts for those on a low-fat diet to a taste of nostalgia for those who remember granny's hot steamed calorie busters. There are delicious chocolate confections, cool cheesecakes, meringues, pies of all persuasions – including American specialities – and a chapter devoted to the apple.

Many countries are justifiably proud of their pies, but there's something special about the American variety – not only are they bigger, better and more luscious than many of their culinary counterparts, but they represent, like the nation itself, a rich diversity of cultures.

I hope you will find all your old favourites in the chapter on traditional puddings. This is the place to find some winter indulgences, satisfying and substantial sweets for when it's cold outside, something you deserve to cheer you up in the greyest weather. The choice can be cheap and cheerful, or rich and wicked.

Glowing colours, pure flavours – fruit has so much to offer the dedicated dessert cook. Those who are worried about the amount of fat in their diet, or are expecting guests who are, should find plenty of inspiration in the fruit chapter.

Ice cream is the classic cooler for hot weather, but don't limit your enjoyment of ices to the summer, as they can provide the ideal ending for a hot, spicy or rich meal at any time of year. Churning the ice cream as it freezes breaks up the ice crystals to give a smoother finish, but you don't have to have a machine before you can turn out home-made ices, all you need is a freezer and an enthusiasm for them.

You don't think that chocolate deserves a chapter all on its own in a pudding book, being just one flavour among many? Come on now, get real, we're talking classic here, the ultimate temptation and most popular flavour; I know, I married a chocoholic. Use the best possible chocolate you can afford, with a high percentage of cocoa solids, as you will immediately notice the difference this makes to the finished dish.

What could be more wholesome, honest, or down-to-earth than an apple? Forget the usual image of Eve's temptation, there is something comforting and homely about any recipe involving this fruit.

I have been lucky enough in my work to travel to many countries to sample the food. There is nothing that brings back the memories of a holiday so quickly and easily as repeating the tastes of the foods first sampled abroad. As for those who have yet to experience the delights of dining under foreign skies, they can say that they may not have visited the country, but they have eaten the pie!

The final chapter should provide some opportunities to show off – and why not? There's a degree of theatricality and showmanship involved whenever we invite people round for a meal, and being able to throw a good party is a matter of congratulation, not censure. Even if you do not entertain often you may find that there are occasions, such as family gatherings, when you have a crowd of people to feed. This chapter gives some examples of puddings that have proved very popular with my family and friends.

Susan Brookes

American Pies

Pumpkin Pie

I think of this as a very American dish, and yet there are old British versions of parsnip and marrow pies, made late in the season when much of the starch in the vegetables has turned to sugar, so this could well be a traditional recipe which the early settlers took to the New World and adapted.

Cut the pumpkin into chunks and spread them out in a large roasting tin. Cover with foil. Bake in a preheated oven, 200°C (400°F), Gas Mark 6, for 45 minutes; this helps to dehydrate the pumpkin and concentrate the flavour. Meanwhile, make the pastry. Mix the flours with the salt in a large bowl. Rub in the margarine until the mixture resembles fine breadcrumbs, then add enough cold water to mix to a firm dough. Roll out the pastry on a lightly floured surface and use to line a 23 cm (9 inch) round flan dish. Prick the base with a fork and chill in the refrigerator until required.

When the pumpkin is cooked, tip into a colander and squeeze out all the excess water by pressing the chunks firmly against the sides of the colander with the back of a wooden spoon. When as much liquid as possible has been removed, purée the pumpkin in a blender or food processor. Transfer the purée to a bowl, add the lime or lemon juice, with the nutmeg, cinnamon and sugar; mix well. Finally stir in the yogurt and beaten eggs.

Pour the filling into the pastry case. Bake in a preheated oven, 190°C (375°F), Gas Mark 5, for 30 minutes. If the filling is not yet golden brown and set, reduce the oven temperature to 180°C (350°F), Gas Mark 4 and bake for 20-30 minutes more.

Serves 6-8

750 G (1½ LB) PUMPKIN, WITHOUT SKIN OR SEEDS

1 TABLESPOON FRESHLY SQUEEZED LIME OR LEMON JUICE

¼ TEASPOON GRATED NUTMEG

¼ TEASPOON GROUND CINNAMON

75 G (3 OZ) SOFT DARK BROWN SUGAR

250 G (8 OZ) GREEK YOGURT

3 EGGS, BEATEN

PASTRY

75 G (3 OZ) PLAIN WHITE FLOUR

75 G (3 OZ) WHOLEMEAL FLOUR

PINCH OF SALT

75 G (3 OZ) MARGARINE

Left: *Pumpkin Pie*

Key Lime Pie

The name comes from the Florida Keys, where some of the world's finest limes are grown. This version, however, was given to me by a German chef living in the Cayman Islands. His tip for keeping the base crisp by coating it with melted chocolate is a good one, and adds to the flavour, too.

CHOCOLATE-COATED CRUMB CRUST

12 DIGESTIVE BISCUITS

75 G (3 OZ) BUTTER

125 G (4 OZ) PLAIN CHOCOLATE, BROKEN INTO SQUARES

FILLING AND TOPPING

3-4 LIMES

3 EGG YOLKS

397 G (14 OZ) CAN CONDENSED MILK

Crumb the biscuits finely, in a food processor, or place in a strong polythene bag and crush with a rolling pin. Melt the butter in a large saucepan, stir in the crumbs, then press the mixture on to the base and sides of a 23 cm (9 inch) round pie dish with sloping sides. Press the crust down well with a spatula or the back of a wooden spoon, then leave to cool in the refrigerator.

Melt the chocolate in a heatproof bowl over a pan of barely simmering water. Stir, then carefully spread the melted chocolate over the cooled crust and set aside to cool again.

Make the filling. Wash the limes to remove any wax coating, then pare 2 of them thinly with a zester. Reserve the pared rind for the topping. Squeeze the limes and reserve 4 tablespoons of the juice.

Whisk the egg yolks in a bowl until pale and fluffy, then beat in the condensed milk and the reserved lime juice. Continue to beat or whisk the mixture until it becomes thick and creamy. Pour into the chocolate-coated crumb crust, then place the pie in the refrigerator and chill until the filling is set. Decorate with the reserved pared lime rind.

Black Satin Pie

This tastes and looks as sensuous as its name, dark, rich, smooth and tasty; in fact, just the thing to round off a romantic dinner.

Make the nut crust. Chop the nuts finely by hand or in a food processor. Melt the butter in a large saucepan, add the chopped nuts, breadcrumbs, sugar and salt and mix well. Press the mixture on to the base and sides of a lightly greased 23 cm (9 inch) round pie dish with sloping sides, pressing down well with a spatula or the back of a wooden spoon. Make a scalloped edge by pinching all round the pie rim with your thumb and index finger.

Bake the pie crust in a preheated oven, 180°C (350°F), Gas Mark 4, for about 15 minutes. If the crust has bubbled up during baking, smooth it back into shape with the back of a metal spoon. Set aside to cool.

Make the filling. Place the milk and chocolate in a large pan and heat gently, stirring occasionally until the chocolate has melted. Meanwhile, mix the corn-flour and measured watertogether in a cup to form a smooth paste. Take the pan off the heat and stir the cornflour paste into the chocolate milk. Return to the heat and bring to the boil, stirring all the time, to form a thick, smooth sauce. Stir the Cointreau or orange juice into the sauce, then pour the filling into the nut crust. Cover to prevent the formation of a skin, and leave to cool.

To decorate the pie, pipe a lattice of whipped cream over the surface and place violet petals at the intersections.

Serves 6

NUT CRUST
125 G (4 OZ) PECAN NUTS

125 G (4 OZ) BUTTER

125 G (4 OZ) FRESH WHITE BREADCRUMBS

75 G (3 OZ) SOFT DARK BROWN SUGAR

$\frac{1}{4}$ TEASPOON SALT

FILLING
300 ML ($\frac{1}{2}$ PINT) MILK

125 G (4 OZ) PLAIN CHOCOLATE, BROKEN INTO SQUARES

I TABLESPOON CORNFLOUR

2 TABLESPOONS WATER

I TABLESPOON COINTREAU OR FRESHLY SQUEEZED ORANGE JUICE

TO DECORATE
150 ML ($\frac{1}{4}$ PINT) DOUBLE CREAM, WHIPPED

15 G ($\frac{1}{2}$ OZ) CRYSTALLIZED VIOLET PETALS

Blueberry Pie

CREAM CHEESE PASTRY

250 G (8 OZ) PLAIN FLOUR

125 G (4 OZ) CREAM CHEESE,
SOFTENED

150 G (5 OZ) BUTTER OR
MARGARINE, SOFTENED

3 TABLESPOONS CASTER SUGAR

FILLING

500 G (1 LB) PREPARED
BLUEBERRIES, THAWED IF
FROZEN

125 G (4 OZ) CASTER SUGAR

2 TABLESPOONS WATER

ICING SUGAR, FOR DUSTING

In America, they are called blueberries, and are bigger than the bilberries I picked as a child on Brimham Rocks. In Scotland you pick blaeberries, but whatever name you know them by, they all dye your mouth purple, so kids can stick their tongues out to scare each other.

Make the cream cheese pastry by putting all the ingredients into a large bowl and mixing together with the fingers of one hand. If the butter and cream cheese are sufficiently soft (they should have been out of the refrigerator for at least 1 hour), the warmth of your hand should be enough to bind the mixture to a fairly soft, smooth pastry.

Wrap one-third of the pastry in greaseproof paper or clingfilm and place in the refrigerator to firm up. Pat out the remaining pastry and use to line a 20 cm (8 inch) round pie dish; leave to cool and firm up in the refrigerator while making the filling. If you want to you can make 4 individual pies using this quantity of pastry. Divide the pastry into 4: pat out and use to line 4 individual 10 cm (4 inch) tartlet tins.

Put the blueberries, caster sugar and measured water in a pan and heat gently until the juices start to run. Using a slotted spoon, transfer the berries to the lined pie dish and fill the pie shell to just below the rim. Reserve any juice.

The reserved pastry should now have firmed sufficiently to be rolled out on a lightly floured surface. Cut into strips about 1 cm (½ inch) wide and cover the top of the pie with a straight or twisted lattice, sealing the ends to the pastry rim with a little water.

Bake in a preheated oven, 190°C (375°F), Gas Mark 5, for 30 minutes or until the pastry is crisp and golden. Dust with icing sugar and serve warm or cold, with the reserved blueberry juice.

Serves 6

Right: *Blueberry Pie*

Banoffee

250 G (8 OZ) GINGERNUT
BISCUITS

275 G (9 OZ) BUTTER

175 G (6 OZ) CASTER SUGAR

397 G (14 OZ) CAN
SWEETENED CONDENSED MILK

150 ML (¼ PINT) DOUBLE
CREAM

3 BANANAS, SLICED

TO DECORATE

2-3 BANANAS

LEMON JUICE

WHIPPED CREAM

GRATED CHOCOLATE

This dessert obviously takes its name from the main ingredients – bananas and toffee (although the origins of the dish are obscure). I used to make the filling by boiling an unopened can of condensed milk, but unless you are very careful, this can result in a nasty accident. Here is a much safer version. The flavour reminds me of South America, and in particular Chile, where the sweet toffee taste is almost a national obsession; chocolate-covered toffee balls, called manjar, are sold at petrol stations, just in case you should be overcome by the desire for it while tootling down the Pan American Highway.

Make the base. Crumb the biscuits in a food processor, or place in a strong polythene bag and crush with a rolling pin. Melt 125 g (4 oz) of the butter in a small saucepan, stir in the crumbs until well coated, then press the mixture on to the base of a 20 cm (8 inch) round loose-bottomed flan tin. Leave to chill in the refrigerator.

Melt the remaining butter and the sugar in a saucepan over a gentle heat. Stir in the condensed milk and the cream. Simmer gently, stirring all the time, for 5 minutes, or until the mixture forms a light golden caramel.

Arrange the sliced bananas over the chilled biscuit base. Pour the caramel over the top and leave to cool. Chill in the refrigerator for several hours or overnight, until set.

To serve, remove the banoffee pie from the tin and transfer it to a chilled serving plate. Slice the bananas into a bowl and toss with a little lemon juice to prevent discoloration. Decorate the pie with whirls of whipped cream, the drained banana slices and a sprinkling of grated chocolate. Serve at once.

Serves 4-6

Bob's Pecan Pie

Everything in America is bigger, even the pecan pies, as I found to my cost when I somehow got into a Pecan Pie Contest with Bob Payton, the American who runs Stapleford Park and a chain of pizza restaurants. Heaven knows how I got myself into such a no-win situation; his version is bigger and better but I offer my variation in case you are unable to get corn syrup (and for all those whose appetites are not quite as big as Bob's).

Whisk the eggs in a large bowl. Add the sugar, melted butter and corn syrup and mix well. Scatter the toasted pecans over the pastry case, pour the filling over the top and then bake in a preheated oven, 180°C (350°F), Gas Mark 4, for 40-50 minutes. Serve warm, with cream.

Serves 8

Variation

For a more modest pie which will serve 6, use a 20 cm (8 inch) round pastry case. Bake blind as before. Whisk 2 eggs in a bowl, then stir in 175 ml (6 fl oz) golden syrup, 125 g (4 oz) soft dark brown sugar and 175 g (6 oz) pecan nuts. Pour the filling into the pastry case. Bake as for the larger pie, but for only about 30 minutes or until set. This pie can be eaten hot or cold, but is delicious when served warm, with a spoonful of vanilla ice cream.

5 EGGS

425 G (14 OZ) SOFT DARK BROWN SUGAR

50 G (2 OZ) BUTTER, MELTED

350 ML (12 FL OZ) LIGHT CORN SYRUP

375 G (12 OZ) PECAN NUTS, TOASTED

30 CM (12 INCH) PASTRY CASE, BAKED BLIND

Mississippi Mud Pie

24 CHOCOLATE CREAM
BISCUITS (BOURBON CREAMS
OR GIPSY CREAMS)

75 G (3 OZ) BUTTER

CHOCOLATE TOPPING

50 G (2 OZ) BUTTER

50 G (2 OZ) PLAIN
CHOCOLATE, BROKEN INTO
SQUARES

2 TABLESPOONS GOLDEN
SYRUP

1 TABLESPOON WATER

FILLING

125 G (4 OZ) PECAN NUTS,
TOASTED

1 LITRE (1¾ PINTS) COFFEE
ICE CREAM

To be honest, there are some dreary desserts masquerading as Mississippi Mud Pie – I've even had some that taste like mud, which is a pity, as it's a good name and a delicious dessert when properly prepared. This version works well, but use a good quality coffee ice cream and remember to toast the pecans.

Grease a deep 20 cm (8 inch) round cake tin. Crumb the biscuits finely in a food processor, or place in a strong polythene bag and crush with a rolling pin. Melt the butter in a large saucepan and stir in the biscuit crumbs until they are well coated. Press the crumb mixture on to the base of the prepared cake tin and chill in the refrigerator until set.

Make the topping. Put the butter, chocolate, golden syrup and measured water in a small saucepan over a low heat until all of the ingredients have melted to form a smooth sauce. Leave to cool.

For the filling, roughly chop the pecan nuts, leaving some large chunks to give texture to the 'mud'. In a large bowl, stir the nuts into the ice cream. Spoon the mixture over the biscuit base, level the surface, then pour over the topping. Cover and freeze for 1 hour (or several weeks if preferred). Transfer the pie to the refrigerator 30 minutes before serving, to soften.

Serves 6

Shoofly Pie

I have always assumed that this pie got its name because the sugar and molasses attracted flies, which had to be shooed away when the pie was cooling. Traditionalists would serve it with cream, but you might like to follow the current American fashion of adding a sharper, less calorific accompaniment such as a fruit salsa. This is simply an uncooked sauce made from fresh fruit (see recipes below).

Roll out the pastry on a lightly floured surface and use to line a 23 cm (9 inch) round pie dish. In a bowl, mix the flour, sugar, cinnamon, ginger, nutmeg and salt together. Rub in the butter until the mixture resembles fine breadcrumbs. Set aside. Mix the water and molasses in a heatproof bowl; stir to combine. Spread half the crumble mixture over the pastry base, pour the molasses over evenly, and then sprinkle the remaining crumble mixture on top. Bake in a preheated oven, 190°C (375°F), Gas Mark 5, for 35-40 minutes, or until set. Cool – keeping any flies shooed away – and serve at room temperature.

Serves 8

Accompaniments

Strawberry Salsa

Hull 250 g (8 oz) strawberries. Put half of them in a blender or food processor, add 3 tablespoons of caster sugar and blend to a smooth purée. Transfer to a bowl. Dice the remaining strawberries and stir into the purée. Cover and chill in the refrigerator until ready to serve.

Melon Salsa

Cut a small melon in half, remove the seeds and scoop the flesh into a blender or food processor. Process briefly, add 2 tablespoons of caster sugar and 1 teaspoon of ground ginger, and process briefly again to produce a chunky purée. Transfer to a bowl, cover and chill in the refrigerator until ready to serve.

250 G (8 OZ) SHORTCRUST
PASTRY (SEE PAGE 37)
300 G (10 OZ) WHOLEMEAL
FLOUR
125 G (4 OZ) DEMERARA
SUGAR
$\frac{1}{4}$ TEASPOON GROUND
CINNAMON
$\frac{1}{4}$ TEASPOON GROUND GINGER
$\frac{1}{4}$ TEASPOON GRATED NUTMEG
$\frac{1}{4}$ TEASPOON SALT
150 G (5 OZ) BUTTER OR
MARGARINE
175 ML (6 FL OZ) BOILING
WATER
125 ML (4 FL OZ) MOLASSES

Banana Cream Pie

CHOCOLATE-COATED CRUMB
CRUST (SEE KEY LIME PIE,
PAGE 12)

FILLING

75 G (3 OZ) SUGAR

1 TABLESPOON CORNFLOUR

450 ML (¾ PINT) MILK

2 EGG YOLKS

1 TEASPOON VANILLA ESSENCE

125 ML (4 FL OZ) DOUBLE
CREAM

4 BANANAS

½ X 142 G (5 OZ) TABLET
LIME JELLY, BROKEN INTO
CUBES

250 ML (8 FL OZ) BOILING
WATER

The first shipment of bananas came into New York from Cuba in 1804. Since then, Americans have come up with dozens of recipes for this nutritious tropical fruit, of which this is one of the earliest and best.

Make the crumb crust in a 23 cm (9 inch) round pie dish. Set aside to cool.

Mix the sugarwith the cornflour in a heatproof bowl. Stir in enough of the milk to mix to a paste, then add the egg yolks and blend until smooth. Heat the rest of the milk in a small saucepan to just below boiling point. Pour the hot milk on to the egg yolk mixture, stirring constantly. Return the mixture to a clean pan and heat gently, stirring all the time until the mixture thickens to a custard-like consistency. Remove from the heat, stir in the vanilla essence, cover and leave to cool.

Whip the cream until it just holds its shape, then fold into the cooled custard. Slice 2 of the bananas over the chocolate-coated crumb crust; pour the custard filling over and smooth the surface. Chill the pie in the refrigerator for about 1-2 hours.

To finish, mix the jelly and boiling water in a heatproof measuring jug. Stir until all the jelly has dissolved. Set aside until cool but not set. Slice the rest of the bananas and arrange in circles over the surface of the pie. Spoon a little of the jelly over the bananas to prevent discoloration and hold them in position; when this is set, add the rest of the jelly glaze. Chill before serving.

Serves 4-6

Mom's Open-Face Apple Pie

'As American as apple pie.' Isn't that how the saying goes? Maybe this is what they mean by it: not too much pastry, sweet and tart with just a hint of spice – it's the sort of pudding that reminds us all of home.

Roll out the pastry on a lightly floured surface and use to line a greased 23 cm (9 inch) round pie dish. Peel and core the apples, then slice into a bowl. Add the sugar, flour, lemon juice, cinnamon, nutmeg and salt and toss to coat well. Arrange the apple slices in the pastry case. Dot with butter. Cover with a sheet of foil. Bake in a preheated oven, 200°C (400°F), Gas Mark 6, for 30 minutes. Remove from the oven, drizzle over the maple syrup, then bake for 10 minutes without the foil covering. The apple should be tender and the pastry golden. Serve hot, warm or cold, with cream or ice cream, if liked.

Serves 8

250 G (8 OZ) SHORTCRUST PASTRY (SEE PAGE 37)
1 KG (2 LB) COOKING APPLES
125 G (4 OZ) SUGAR
2 TABLESPOONS PLAIN FLOUR
1 TABLESPOON LEMON JUICE
½ TEASPOON GROUND CINNAMON
¼ TEASPOON GRATED NUTMEG
PINCH OF SALT
25 G (1 OZ) BUTTER, DICED
1 TABLESPOON MAPLE SYRUP

Chocolate Peanut Butter Pie

Line and grease a 23 cm (9 inch) round pie dish. Crumb the peanut biscuits in a food processor, or place in a strong polythene bag and crush with a rolling pin. Melt the butter in a saucepan, stir in the crumbs and mix well. Press the mixture on to the base of the dish and chill in the refrigerator, until set.
Mix the cornflour and measured water together to form a smooth paste. Put the milk and chocolate in a saucepan and stir over a low heat until melted and smooth. Pour on to the cornflour paste, stirring, then return to a clean pan. Heat, stirring constantly until the mixture boils and thickens. Remove from the heat, add the peanut butter and beat until smoothly blended. Pour the filling on to the base. Sprinkle with the chopped peanuts. Serve warm or cold.

Serves 8

12 LARGE PEANUT BISCUITS
75 G (3 OZ) BUTTER
1 TABLESPOON CORNFLOUR
3 TABLESPOONS WATER
300 ML (½ PINT) MILK
125 G (4 OZ) PLAIN CHOCOLATE, BROKEN INTO SQUARES
2 TABLESPOONS SMOOTH PEANUT BUTTER
25 G (1 OZ) ROASTED PEANUTS, CHOPPED

Down Home Peach Pie

500 G (1 LB) PUFF PASTRY,
THAWED IF FROZEN

1 EGG, BEATEN

2 X 425 G (14 OZ) CANS
SLICED PEACHES

1 TABLESPOON ARROWROOT

1 TEASPOON GROUND
CINNAMON

2 TABLESPOONS LEMON JUICE

2 TABLESPOONS WATER

WHIPPED CREAM, TO SERVE

Just saying the name of this pie makes my mouth water. Somehow it reminds me of Elvis. It may be the sign of a misspent youth, or just that this is particularly associated with the Southern States. You can make it with fresh peaches, but it works equally well with canned fruit.

Roll out the pastry on a lightly floured surface and use to line a greased 25 cm (10 inch) round quiche dish. Trim the pastry generously around the edge of the dish so that the surplus can be folded over to make a double rim. Cut leaves from the pastry trimmings to make a decorative border to set along this rim. Prick the base of the pie shell with a fork, then add some crumpled foil to support the sides of the pie shell while baking blind.

Bake the shell in a preheated oven, 200°C (400°F), Gas Mark 6, for 15 minutes until the pastry is set, then remove the foil, brush the pie shell with the beaten egg and return to the oven for 10 minutes more. Cool slightly.

Drain the peaches, reserving the juice in a small saucepan. In a bowl, mix the arrowroot, cinnamon, lemon juice and measured water together to form a paste. Heat the peach syrup gently. Stir in the arrowroot paste and bring the mixture to the boil. When it clears, cook for 30 seconds more, then remove from the heat and leave to cool slightly.

Arrange the peach slices in the pie shell, spoon the thickened peach syrup over the top and set aside to cool to room temperature. Serve the pie in slices, with a spoonful of whipped cream on each portion.

Serves 6-8

Right: *Down Home Peach Pie*

Black Bottom Pie

24 GINGERNUT BISCUITS

75 G (3 OZ) BUTTER OR MARGARINE

50 G (2 OZ) SOFT BROWN SUGAR

50 G (2 OZ) PLAIN CHOCOLATE, BROKEN INTO SQUARES

11 G (½ OZ) SACHET POWDERED GELATINE

3 TABLESPOONS WATER

1 TABLESPOON CORNFLOUR

125 G (4 OZ) GRANULATED SUGAR

300 ML (½ PINT) MILK

3 EGGS, SEPARATED

1 TEASPOON VANILLA ESSENCE

1 TABLESPOON RUM

TO DECORATE

125 ML (4 FL OZ) DOUBLE CREAM

1 TABLESPOON COCOA POWDER

The name comes from the dark chocolate base: I don't think it has anything to do with the dance of the same name, although both seem to have their origins early this century.

Grease a 20 cm (8 inch) round loose-bottomed cake tin. Crumb the biscuits in a food processor, or place in a strong polythene bag and crush with a rolling pin. Melt the butter or margarine with the brown sugar in a saucepan over a gentle heat, add the biscuit crumbs and mix well. Press the mixture on to the base of the tin and chill in the refrigerator until set.

Melt the chocolate in a heatproof bowl over barely simmering water. In a small bowl, sprinkle the gelatine on to the measured water. Set aside until spongy, then set the bowl over simmering water until the gelatine has dissolved.

Mix the cornflour, half the sugar with a little of the milk to form a paste. Stir in the dissolved gelatine. Place the remaining milk in a saucepan. Add the egg yolks and whisk in the gelatine mixture. Heat slowly, stirring all the time, until the custard thickens sufficiently to coat the back of a wooden spoon.

Divide the custard between 2 bowls. Stir the melted chocolate and vanilla essence into 1 bowl, then cover both bowls and set aside to cool. As soon as the chocolate-flavoured custard starts to set, pour it over the crumb base and chill. Whisk the egg whites in a grease-free bowl until stiff, then gradually add the remaining sugar, whisking until firm and glossy. Add the rum to the remaining custard mixture, then fold in the beaten egg whites. Pile into the cake tin, over the chocolate layer. Level the surface. Refrigerate for several hours, or overnight, until set.

To serve, remove the pie from the tin and transfer to a plate. Whip the cream and put into a piping bag fitted with a shell nozzle. Decorate with whirls of cream and sift a light dusting of cocoa over the top.

Serves 8-10

Butterscotch Meringue Pie

Roll out the pastry on a lightly floured surface and use to line a 23 cm (9 inch) round pie dish. Mix the egg yolks, sugar, cornflour and 4 tablespoons of the milk to form a paste. Heat the remaining milk to just below boiling point, then pour on to the cornflour mixture, stirring all the time. Return to a clean pan and heat, stirring, until the custard thickens. Off the heat, stir in the butter and vanilla essence until the butter has melted. Pour into the pastry case and cool. Whisk the egg whites in a grease-free bowl until stiff; gradually whisk in the sugar until firm and glossy. Spread over the filling, taking the meringue right to the edges to form a seal. Use the back of a spoon to lift the meringue into peaks. Bake in a preheated oven, 200°C (400°F), Gas Mark 6, for 15 minutes or until crisp and lightly browned. Cool to room temperature before serving.

Serves 8

250 G (8 OZ) SHORTCRUST
PASTRY (SEE PAGE 37)
2 EGGS, SEPARATED
250 G (8 OZ) SOFT DARK
BROWN SUGAR
3 TABLESPOONS CORNFLOUR
600 ML (1 PINT) MILK
25 G (1 OZ) BUTTER, DICED
1 TEASPOON VANILLA ESSENCE
175 G (6 OZ) CASTER SUGAR

Pennsylvania Funnel Cakes

Mix the flour, milk, almond essence and egg together to form a batter. The batter should be well blended and smooth, as for Yorkshire pudding. If lumps develop, simply rub through a sieve into a clean bowl.

Heat the oil to 180°C (350°F) or until a cube of bread browns in 30 seconds. Pour one-sixth of the batter into a funnel, holding your finger over the end of the funnel to prevent it from running out. Release a thin stream of batter into the hot oil in a spiral going outwards from the centre, practice makes perfect as with pancakes. Fry for 3 minutes until golden on one side, flip over, and cook for 2 minutes on the other side. Drain well on kitchen paper, and dredge with icing sugar. Keep warm while making 5 more funnel cakes in the same way. Serve at once.

Serves 6

175 G (6 OZ) SELF-RAISING
FLOUR
175 ML (6 FL OZ) MILK
1 TEASPOON ALMOND ESSENCE
1 EGG
OIL, FOR DEEP-FRYING
ICING SUGAR, FOR DREDGING

Traditional Puddings

Sticky Toffee Puddings

I must warn you that the puddings are so delicious that I have never been able to keep half for another day; guests always want seconds.

Arrange paper muffin cases in an 8-hole muffin tin. Alternatively, use paper bun cases in a 12-hole bun tin and reduce the cooking time by 5 minutes. If the dates are large, dice them into even-sized pieces, then put them in a heatproof bowl with the coffee. Pour the boiling water over them, mix, and leave to soak and cool for about 10 minutes.

Cream the butter and sugar together in a bowl until light and fluffy. Add a teaspoon of the flour to prevent curdling, then beat in a small amount of the beaten eggs. Continue adding alternate amounts of flour and egg until all have been added. This will make a firm cake mixture. Stir in the date and coffee mixture, mix well, then divide between the paper muffin or bun cases.

Bake in a preheated oven, 180°C (350°F), Gas Mark 4, for 30 minutes or until well risen and springy to the touch. Transfer the puddings in the paper cases to a wire rack to cool.

Make the toffee sauce. Combine the butter, brown sugar and cream in a pan. Heat gently until both the butter and the sugar have melted. Simmer, stirring, for 2 minutes or until the mixture looks like thin toffee.

To serve, peel the paper off each warm pudding and place in individual dishes. Pour the toffee sauce over and around each pudding. A little cream may be poured over the puddings in addition to the toffee sauce, if liked.

Serves 8 (6 if using bun tins)

125 G (4 OZ) CHOPPED DATES

1 TABLESPOON INSTANT COFFEE GRANULES

150 ML (¼ PINT) BOILING WATER

50 G (2 OZ) BUTTER

75 G (3 OZ) SOFT BROWN SUGAR

150 G (5 OZ) SELF-RAISING FLOUR

2 EGGS, BEATEN

TOFFEE SAUCE

125 G (4 OZ) BUTTER

175 G (6 OZ) SOFT BROWN SUGAR

150 ML (¼ PINT) SINGLE CREAM

Left: Sticky Toffee Puddings

Spotted Dick

150 ML (¼ PINT) MILK

I TABLESPOON TREACLE OR
GOLDEN SYRUP

75 G (3 OZ) SELF-RAISING
FLOUR

125 G (4 OZ) FRESH BROWN
BREADCRUMBS

50 G (2 OZ) SOFT BROWN
SUGAR

75 G (3 OZ) SHREDDED SUET

¼ TEASPOON MIXED SPICE

125 G (4 OZ) MIXED
DRIED FRUIT

50 G (2 OZ) WALNUTS,
CHOPPED

50 G (2 OZ) GLACÉ CHERRIES,
HALVED

Some people call this rich, fruity steamed pudding spotted dog, which I suppose is less likely to cause giggles around the dining table. Serve it with custard for every day, or with cream whisked with a little Cointreau for a special occasion. This is a modern version of a very old recipe, which can be made and cooked very quickly if you have a microwave.

Lightly oil or grease a 1.2 litre (2 pint) pudding basin. Put the milk and treacle or golden syrup in a small saucepan and heat gently, stirring, until smooth. Leave to cool slightly.

Combine the remaining ingredients in a mixing bowl and mix well. Beat in the sweetened milk, then spoon the mixture into the prepared pudding basin. Cover with a piece of buttered foil which has been pleated in the centre to allow the pudding to rise. Tie with string.

Place a trivet or upturned saucer in a large saucepan, add the pudding and pour in boiling water to come halfway up the basin sides. Allow the water to return to the boil, then lower the heat and simmer for 1½-2 hours, topping up the water as required.

Alternatively, cook the pudding in a microwave oven. Spoon the mixture into a suitable basin, cover loosely with microwave film and cook on High for 5½ minutes. Leave to stand for 5 minutes. Turn the pudding out on to a plate and serve at once.

Serves 4

Steamed Syrup Pudding

This is the classic hot, filling winter pudding that many people remember from their schooldays. In the past, it was always made with shredded suet rather than butter, and suet may be used in this recipe if you wish. However, butter gives a lighter texture and, in my opinion, a nicer taste.

Grease a 1 litre (1¾ pint) pudding basin with 15 g (½ oz) of the butter and put the golden syrup in the base. Cream the remaining butter and sugar together in a bowl, until pale and fluffy, then add the eggs, a little at a time, alternately with the flour. Stir in enough milk to give a soft dropping consistency.

Spoon this mixture over the syrup in the prepared pudding basin. and cover with a piece of buttered foil which has been pleated in the centre to allow the pudding to rise. Tie with string.

Stand the pudding basin on a trivet or upturned saucer in a large saucepan, and pour in boiling water to about 4 cm (1½ inches) from the top of the basin. Allow the water to return to the boil, then lower the heat and simmer for 1½ hours, topping up the water as required. Let the pudding stand for about 5 minutes, then run a knife around the inside of the basin. Turn the pudding out on to a serving plate and serve at once.

Serves 4

Variations

Maple syrup, jam or marmalade may be used instead of golden syrup. To make a fruity sponge, stir 50 g (2 oz) sultanas into the pudding mixture.

140 G (4½ OZ) BUTTER

3 TABLESPOONS GOLDEN SYRUP

125 G (4 OZ) CASTER SUGAR

2 EGGS, BEATEN

125 G (4 OZ) SELF-RAISING FLOUR

ABOUT 2 TABLESPOONS MILK

Crème Caramel

600 ML (I PINT) MILK

2 EGGS, PLUS 2 EGG YOLKS

2 TABLESPOONS CASTER SUGAR

150 ML (¼ PINT) EVAPORATED

MILK

125 G (4 OZ) GRANULATED

SUGAR

150 ML (¼ PINT) WATER

This simple classic remains one of the world's most popular puddings.

Heat the milk to lukewarm in a saucepan or in a jug in the microwave. Beat the eggs and egg yolks together in a large bowl, add the caster sugar and evaporated milk and whisk until all the sugar has dissolved. Stir the lukewarm milk into the mixture.

Warm the granulated sugar with the measured water until all the sugar has dissolved, then raise the heat and boil the mixture without stirring until it turns a golden brown caramel colour. Pour the mixture into a warmed 1 litre (1¾ pint) ovenproof dish, swirling the caramel around to cover as much of the base and sides of the dish as possible.

Pour the milk and egg mixture carefully into the dish, over the back of a wooden spoon, so that the caramel is undisturbed.

Cover the dish with foil or greaseproof paper and put it in a bain marie (a roasting tin half full of hot water). Bake in a preheated oven, 180°C (350°F), Gas Mark 4, for 1 hour, by which time the custard should have set. Crème Caramel may be served warm, straight from the dish, or turned out on to a platter when quite cold.

Serves 4

Apricot & Almond Trifle

This trifle benefits from being made a few hours, or even a day before, you are planning to serve it, so that the flavours can develop and mingle. The flavour of the almonds is much improved if they are toasted, either under a grill or in a hot oven. Watch them carefully, and remove them as soon as they start to brown – it is very easy to forget them and burn the lot.

First make the custard sauce. Whisk the egg yolks and caster sugar together in a bowl until the mixture is thick and the whisk leaves a trail when lifted. Heat the milk in a saucepan to just below boiling point, then pour a little of the milk on to the egg mixture, stirring all the time. Stir in the rest of the milk gradually, then pour the mixture back into a clean pan. Heat gently, stirring all the time, until the mixture thickens sufficiently to coat the back of a wooden spoon. Take care not to allow the custard to boil or it will curdle. Remove from the heat and stir in the vanilla essence. Cover the custard and leave to cool, when it will thicken further.

Prepare the trifle. Crumble half the trifle sponges into the base of a large glass bowl. Sprinkle with 2 tablespoons of the Amaretto. Purée the apricots with about half the juice from the can in a blender or food processor.

Spread half the apricot purée over the soaked sponges in small spoonfuls, then cover with a little less than half the cooked custard sauce. Repeat the layers.

Whip the cream in a bowl until thick enough to hold its shape; spread over the top of the trifle, then sprinkle with the toasted flaked almonds.

Serves 8

375 G (12 OZ) TRIFLE SPONGES

4 TABLESPOONS AMARETTO

397 G (14 OZ) CAN APRICOT HALVES IN NATURAL JUICE

300 ML (½ PINT) DOUBLE CREAM

50 G (2 OZ) FLAKED ALMONDS, TOASTED

CUSTARD SAUCE

4 EGG YOLKS

5 TABLESPOONS CASTER SUGAR

450 ML (¾ PINT) MILK

1 TEASPOON VANILLA ESSENCE

Atholl Brose

3 TABLESPOONS MEDIUM
OATMEAL

125 G (4 OZ) FRESH
RASPBERRIES (OPTIONAL)

300 ML (½ PINT)
DOUBLE CREAM

1 TABLESPOON CLEAR HONEY

2 TABLESPOONS WHISKY

There are many variations on this old Scottish recipe, I don't think mine is especially authentic, but my Scottish friends seem to like it. It is very rich, and the quantities here will probably serve 6 less-than-hearty-Northern appetites.

Toast the oatmeal in a dry frying pan over a moderate heat until golden brown, stirring all the time with a wooden spoon. Set aside to cool.

If using the raspberries, divide them between 4-6 serving dishes. Whip the cream, honey and whisky in a bowl until thick. Fold in all but 1 tablespoon of the toasted oatmeal, then spoon over the raspberries in the serving dishes.

Sprinkle the remaining oatmeal on top and chill before serving.

Serves 4-6

Rich Rice Pudding

25 G (1 OZ) BUTTER

50 G (2 OZ) SHORT-GRAIN
(PUDDING) RICE

25 G (1 OZ) SUGAR

600 ML (1 PINT) MILK

1 TEASPOON GRATED NUTMEG

*Baked slowly, so that every grain is plump and flavoursome,
rice pudding is one of life's pleasures.*

Use some of the butter to grease a shallow 600 ml (1 pint) ovenproof dish. Spread the rice and sugar over the base of the dish, then pour the milk over. Allow the mixture to stand and soak for about 2 hours (more if possible), then sprinkle the grated nutmeg over the top.

Dot with the remaining butter and bake in a preheated oven, 150°C (300°F), Gas Mark 2, for 2½ hours.

Serves 4

Lemon Posset
with Almond Biscuits

First make the almond biscuits. Line a baking sheet with nonstick baking paper. Cream the butter and the sugar together in a bowl, until pale and fluffy. Stir in the flour and salt and mix well, then stir in the slivered almonds.

Put 6 teaspoons of the mixture spaced well apart, on the prepared baking sheet. Bake in a preheated oven, 200°C (400°F), Gas Mark 6, for about 6-8 minutes until the biscuit edges are tinged with brown. The biscuits spread a lot during cooking and should be allowed to cool a little before being transferred to wire racks. They will crisp as they cool. Continue baking 6 at a time until all the mixture has been used. If not serving immediately, store in an airtight tin.

Make the posset. Combine the cream, sugar, sherry and lemon juice in a bowl. Whisk together until thick. Spoon into 6 wine glasses or stemmed glass dishes and chill in the refrigerator for at least 2 hours.

Serve the posset with a few of the almond biscuits. Offer any of the remaining biscuits separately.

Serves 6

300 ML (½ PINT) DOUBLE CREAM

125 G (4 OZ) CASTER SUGAR

4 TABLESPOONS SHERRY

3 TABLESPOONS LEMON JUICE

ALMOND BISCUITS

75 G (3 OZ) BUTTER, SOFTENED

75 G (3 OZ) CASTER SUGAR

50 G (2 OZ) PLAIN FLOUR

PINCH OF SALT

75 G (3 OZ) FLAKED ALMONDS, CHOPPED INTO FINE SLIVERS

Overleaf, Left: *Lemon Posset with Almond Biscuits*
Right: *Frangipane*

Frangipane

300 G (10 OZ) PUFF PASTRY,
THAWED IF FROZEN
2 TABLESPOONS APRICOT JAM
125 G (4 OZ) BUTTER,
SOFTENED
125 G (4 OZ) CASTER SUGAR
2 EGGS, BEATEN
125 G (4 OZ) GROUND
ALMONDS

There have been different versions of this recipe, thickened with ground almonds, for hundreds of years. This one can be served hot or cold, and, with its lattice top is pretty enough to serve for a dinner party.

Set aside a small amount of pastry for the lattice. Roll out the rest on a lightly floured surface and use to line a 20 cm (8 inch) round flan tin or pie dish. Set the trimmings aside with the reserved pastry. Spread the apricot jam over the pastry base.

Cream the butter and sugar together in a bowl, until pale and fluffy. Add the beaten eggs gradually, then mix in the ground almonds. Spread the mixture evenly over the jam in the pastry case.

Roll out the reserved pastry with the trimmings and cut out long narrow strips. Arrange these in a lattice over the top of the pie, sealing the ends to the pastry rim with a little water.

Bake in a preheated oven, 190°C (375°F), Gas Mark 5, for 45 minutes or until the filling is risen, golden brown and just set.

Serves 6

Cumberland Rum Nicky

A rich dried fruit filling spiked with rum makes this tart the perfect choice for winter evenings.

Make the pastry. Sift the flour and salt into a mixing bowl. Cut in the butter, then rub it in until the mixture resembles fine breadcrumbs. Add enough cold water (about 2 tablespoons) to mix to a dough. Press the dough together to form a ball and knead lightly.

Roll out most of the pastry on a lightly floured surface and use to line a deep 18 cm (7 inch) round flan dish. Melt the butter over a low heat in a saucepan, then add the dried fruit and sugar. Stir over a very low heat until the sugar has melted. Take the pan off the heat and add the rum, mixed spice and lemon juice. Stir well, then tip the mixture into the pastry case. Level the surface.

Roll out the remaining pastry and cut into thin strips. Lay these over the filling in a lattice pattern, sealing the ends to the pastry rim with a little water.

Bake in a preheated oven, 180°C (350°F), Gas Mark 4, for 30-40 minutes. Sprinkle a little caster sugar over the surface of the tart while still warm. Serve hot or cold.

Serves 6

Note

The rule-of-thumb when making basic shortcrust pastry is to use half fat to flour, so for 175 g (6 oz) pastry, you require 175 g (6 oz) plain flour and 75 g (3 oz) fat.

50 G (2 OZ) BUTTER

375 G (12 OZ) MIXED DRIED FRUIT, PREFERABLY INCLUDING MIXED PEEL

50 G (2 OZ) SOFT BROWN SUGAR

3 TABLESPOONS RUM

½ TEASPOON MIXED SPICE

2 TEASPOONS LEMON JUICE

CASTER SUGAR, TO DECORATE

SHORTCRUST PASTRY

250 G (8 OZ) PLAIN FLOUR (SEE NOTE)

PINCH OF SALT

125 G (4 OZ) MARGARINE OR HALF BUTTER AND HALF VEGETABLE FAT

Bread & Butter Pudding

8 LARGE SLICES OF LIGHTLY
BUTTERED BREAD, CRUSTS
REMOVED, HALVED

25 G (1 OZ) SULTANAS

2 EGGS

170 G (6 OZ) CAN
EVAPORATED MILK

450 ML (¾ PINT) MILK

3 TABLESPOONS SUGAR

2 TABLESPOONS FRESH WHITE
BREADCRUMBS

½ TEASPOON GROUND
CINNAMON

This delicious pudding was originally created as a way of using up stale bread. Serve it hot with cream, ice cream or even custard. If you want this to rise up like a soufflé, use a straight-sided dish; a round one about 18 cm (7 inches) in diameter is ideal, and will give a very light result.

Put the slices of bread and butter, with a few sultanas between each layer, in a large ovenproof dish, filling it to within 2.5 cm (1 inch) of the top.

In a large mixing bowl, whisk the eggs, evaporated milk and milk with about 2 tablespoons of the sugar. Pour the mixture over the slices of bread and butter in the dish and leave to soak for at least 1 hour.

Mix the breadcrumbs, cinnamon and the remaining sugar in a bowl; sprinkle this mixture over the top of the pudding. Cover the dish with foil. Bake the pudding in a preheated oven, 140°C (275°F), Gas Mark 1, for 1 hour.

Remove the foil covering and raise the oven temperature to 160°C (325°F), Gas Mark 3. Return the pudding to the oven and bake for 30 minutes more, or until it is well risen and golden brown on top. Serve hot.

Serves 4-6

Right; *Bread and Butter Pudding*

Sussex Pond Pudding

175 G (6 OZ) SELF-RAISING

FLOUR

¼ TEASPOON SALT

75 G (3 OZ) SHREDDED SUET

ABOUT 125 ML (4 FL OZ)

WATER

75 G (3 OZ) BUTTER, FLAKED

75 G (3 OZ) DEMERARA SUGAR

I LEMON

I didn't believe this recipe would work when I first heard about it, and still don't know why it is said to come from Sussex. It is the only recipe I know where you eat a whole lemon, rind and all, and it is well worth trying. Although it is rich, the sharp lemon flavour cuts across the butter and sugar.

Lightly grease a 1 litre (1¾ pint) pudding basin. Mix the flour, salt and suet and in a large bowl with enough water to form a soft dough. Set aside a quarter of the dough for a lid. Roll out the rest on a well floured surface and use to line the pudding basin.

Put a few flakes of the butter and a little of the sugar in the base of the basin, wash the lemon and prick over with a fork, piercing the skin and pith. Add the lemon to the basin and fill the space around it with the rest of the flaked butter and sugar.

Roll out the reserved dough to make a lid. Moisten the edges of the pastry with a little water and press the lid into place, tucking in any overlapping edges. The pudding is now ready to be cooked by one of the following methods:

Steaming: Cover the pudding basin with a piece of buttered foil, which has been pleated in the centre to allow the pudding to rise. Tie with string. Place a trivet or upturned saucer in a large pan, add the pudding and pour in boiling water to come halfway up the basin sides. Return to the boil, then lower the heat and simmer for 2½ hours, topping up the water as required.

Microwave Cooking: Cover a suitable basin loosely with microwave film and cook on High for 9-10 minutes. Stand for 10 minutes before turning out.

Pressure Cooking: Follow the instructions in your manufacturer's handbook for a steamed pudding of similar size.

Leave the pudding to for 5 minutes. If cooked in a saucepan or pressure cooker, before turning out on to a plate. Serve with cream, if liked.

Serves 6

Lemon Meringue Pie

This is one of those puddings that has practically become a cliché. At one time it appeared on almost every restaurant menu. Synthetic-tasting mixes led to its decline, which is a pity, because the combination of fresh citrus and meringue can be absolutely delicious.

Roll out the pastry on a lightly floured surface and use to line a 20 cm (8 inch) round flan dish. Prick the base of the pastry case with a fork, cover with a piece of greaseproof paper and add baking beans or crumpled foil. Bake the case in a preheated oven, 200°C (400°F), Gas Mark 6, for 15 minutes, then remove the beans or foil and return to the oven for another 5 minutes to crisp the base. Leave to cool.

Make the filling. Put the pared lemon rind and measured water in a saucepan and bring to the boil. Blend the lemon juice with the cornflour in a heatproof bowl to form a smooth paste. Pour the boiling water and lemon rind on to the cornflour paste, stirring all the time, then return this mixture to a clean pan and bring to the boil. Lower the heat and simmer for about 1 minute, stirring constantly; the mixture will thicken.

Off the heat, add 75 g (3 oz) of the sugar and the egg yolks. Beat well, then return the pan to a gentle heat and stir the mixture until it has thickened. Cool slightly before spooning the filling into the pastry case.

Make the meringue topping. Whisk the egg whites in a grease-free bowl until stiff peaks form, then beat in the remaining sugar and beat again until firm and glossy. Spread this over the lemon filling, making sure to create a good seal, otherwise the meringue may 'weep'.

Bake in a preheated oven, 160°C (325°F), Gas Mark 3, for 20-30 minutes, until the meringue is crisp on top and starting to brown at the edges. Serve the pie warm or cold.

Serves 6-8

175 G (6 OZ) SHORTCRUST PASTRY (SEE PAGE 37)
THINLY PARED RIND AND JUICE OF 2 LARGE LEMONS
300 ML (½ PINT) WATER
45 G (1½ OZ) CORNFLOUR
200 G (7 OZ) CASTER SUGAR
2 EGGS, SEPARATED

Treacle Tart

Not the most slimming of puddings, this, but a perennial favourite.
Treacle Tart may be eaten hot or cold, but I think it is best just warm,
with cream or custard sauce.

175 G (6 OZ) SHORTCRUST
PASTRY (SEE PAGE 37)
2 TEASPOONS LEMON JUICE
8 TABLESPOONS GOLDEN
SYRUP
50 G (2 OZ) FRESH WHITE
BREADCRUMBS

Roll out the pastry on a lightly floured surface and use to line a 20 cm (8 inch) round flan tin or pie dish. Put the lemon juice, golden syrup and breadcrumbs into a small pan. Heat gently until the syrup has thinned enough to enable all the ingredients to be combined.

Pour the filling into the pastry shell. Bake in a preheated oven, 190°C (375°F), Gas Mark 5, for 30 minutes. Serve hot or cold.

Serves 4-6

Yorkshire Curd Tart

This traditional tart is usually eaten cold or at room temperature. Serve it in
slices, with cream if liked.

175 G (6 OZ) SHORTCRUST
PASTRY (SEE PAGE 37)
1 LEMON
2 TEASPOONS MIXED PEEL
2 EGGS
250 G (8 OZ) CURD OR
COTTAGE CHEESE
50 G (2 OZ) SUGAR
50 G (2 OZ) CURRANTS
¼ TEASPOON GROUND
CINNAMON
¼ TEASPOON GRATED
NUTMEG

Roll out the pastry on a lightly floured surface and use to line a 20 cm (8 inch) round flan tin or pie dish.

Finely grate the rind from the lemon, then finely chop the mixed peel. Beat the eggs in a large mixing bowl, add all the other ingredients including the lemon rind and mixed peel and mix well. Pour the mixture into the pastry case.

Bake in a preheated oven, 180°C (350°F), Gas Mark 4, for 35-50 minutes or until the filling is golden and set. Serve with cream or ice cream, if liked.

Serves 4-6

Gipsy Tart

This has a taste that suggests toffee – or caramel – and appeals to all those with a very sweet tooth.

Roll out the pastry on a lightly floured surface and use to line a 20 cm (8 inch) round flan tin or pie dish. Mix the sugar and condensed milk in a bowl, then stir into the pastry case.

Bake in a preheated oven, 180°C (350°F), Gas Mark 4, for 20 minutes, by which time the filling should be just about set; it firms as it cools.

Serve the tart warm, in slices, or leave to cool and decorate with whirls of whipped cream.

Serves 6

250 G (8 OZ) SHORTCRUST
PASTRY (SEE PAGE 37)
175 G (6 OZ) SOFT BROWN
SUGAR
397 G (14 OZ) CAN
SWEETENED CONDENSED MILK
WHIPPED CREAM, TO
DECORATE

Jam Roly Poly

We used to call this dead man's leg at school, a horribly graphic description. It was always steamed, but I find that baking is not only quicker, but gives a nice crisp crust.

Combine the flour, salt and suet in a large bowl. Mix together with a fork, adding just enough cold water to make a soft dough. Turn out on to a lightly floured surface, and roll out to a 23 cm (9 inch) square. Dot the jam over the surface, then spread it evenly, almost to the edges. Roll the dough up like a Swiss roll and tuck the ends under slightly to seal them.

Put the roll, with the join underneath, on a large baking sheet. Brush the top with a little milk. Bake in a preheated oven, 200°C (400°F), Gas Mark 6, for about 25 minutes. Serve with custard, or with a little more warmed jam poured over the top.

Serves 4

125 G (4 OZ) SELF-RAISING
FLOUR
$\frac{1}{4}$ TEASPOON SALT
50 G (2 OZ) SHREDDED SUET
4 TABLESPOONS RASPBERRY OR
STRAWBERRY JAM
MILK, TO GLAZE

Queen of Puddings

50 G (2 OZ) BUTTER

600 ML (1 PINT) MILK

150 G (5 OZ) BREADCRUMBS

1 TEASPOON LEMON JUICE

150 G (5 OZ) CASTER SUGAR

6 EGGS, SEPARATED

4 TABLESPOONS STRAWBERRY
OR RASPBERRY JAM

This pudding is a good old family favourite, ideal for making when you have little in the larder. I remember it with great affection from my childhood.

Grease or lightly oil a shallow ovenproof dish. Heat the butter and milk together in a large saucepan until the butter has melted and the mixture is lukewarm. Combine the breadcrumbs, lemon juice and 25 g (1 oz) of the sugar in a heatproof bowl; pour the warm milk mixture over. Leave the mixture to stand for 2-3 minutes, then beat the egg yolks into the mixture.

Pour into the prepared dish and bake in a preheated oven, 180°C (350°F), Gas Mark 4, for 30 minutes, by which time it should be just set. Take the pudding out of the oven to allow it to cool a little, which will make the finishing easier. Leave the oven on.

Make the meringue mixture. Whisk the egg whites in a grease-free bowl until stiff, then gradually whisk in the remaining sugar, until the meringue is firm and glossy. Warm the jam to make it easier to spread; carefully smooth it over the surface of the pudding.

Spread the meringue mixture over the jam, sealing well to the sides of the dish. Return the pudding to the oven for 10-12 minutes until the meringue is golden brown. Serve at once.

Serves 4-6

Bakewell Pudding

Although this turns out more like a tart, I'm told by the Derbyshire lass who gave me the recipe that it must always be called pudding. The quantities below yield two 20 cm (8 inch) round puddings; one for immediate consumption and the other for the freezer. Bakewell Pudding freezes well when cooled.

Roll out the pastry on a lightly floured surface and use to line 2 x 20 cm (8 inch) round pie dishes. Spread the jam over the base of each. Melt the butter in a pan, or in a jug in the microwave, then pour into a bowl and leave to cool a little. Beat the eggs in a bowl, then stir in the butter and sugar. Add the ground almonds, stir well, then divide between the pastry cases.

Bake in a preheated oven, 200°C (400°F), Gas Mark 6, for 10 minutes, then reduce the oven temperature to 160°C (325°F), Gas Mark 3, and bake for a further 15 minutes or until set. Serve hot or warm, but not cold.

Each pudding serves 4-6

425 G (14 OZ) SHORTCRUST PASTRY (SEE PAGE 37)
3 TABLESPOONS RASPBERRY JAM
250 G (8 OZ) BUTTER
3 EGGS
250 G (8 OZ) CASTER SUGAR
125 G (4 OZ) GROUND ALMONDS

Semolina

Grease or lightly oil a shallow ovenproof dish. Heat the milk and salt in a pan until lukewarm, then sprinkle the semolina over the surface. Cook, stirring constantly, for 5 minutes, by which time the mixture should be thick and the grains of semolina are clear. Take the pan off the heat and stir in the sugar until dissolved. Beat in the egg yolks and then leave to cool slightly.

Whisk the egg whites in a grease-free bowl until stiff; fold into the semolina mixture. Spoon into the dish and level the surface. Bake in a preheated oven, 180°C (350°F), Gas Mark 4, for 15-20 minutes or until golden on top. Serve with a little grated nutmeg, lemon rind or clear honey drizzled over the top.

Serves 3-4

450 ML (¾ PINT) MILK
¼ TEASPOON SALT
25 G (1 OZ) SEMOLINA
25 G (1 OZ) SUGAR
2 EGGS, SEPARATED

Fruit Desserts

Stuffed Figs

Figs are associated with fruitfulness and the mother figure, because they have so many seeds. This is one of the simplest ways to serve them. Always serve fresh figs at room temperature as refrigerating disguises their delicious flavour. Figs are available in various colours, from pale green to purple. Always look for dry, slightly soft, unblemished fruit. If overripe the skin shrinks.

12 FRESH FIGS

50 G (2 OZ) WALNUTS

3 TABLESPOONS CLEAR HONEY

3 TABLESPOONS SHERRY

125 G (4 OZ) FROMAGE FRAIS

Prepare the figs. Wipe the fruit with a damp cloth if necessary. Ensure that they will stand upright by taking a thin slice off the base of each if required. Snip off any tough stalks, then cut a deep cross in the top of each fruit. Ease the fruit apart slightly to reveal a central pocket for the filling.

Make the stuffing. Finely chop or grind the walnuts, either by hand or in a food processor. Tip the nuts into a large bowl and mix in the honey, sherry and fromage frais to make a stiff mixture.

Spoon a little of the walnut stuffing into the centre of each fig, arrange the stuffed figs on a shallow serving platter (on a bed of fig leaves, if available) and chill before serving.

Serves 6

Left: *Stuffed Figs*

Minted Melon

I SMALL GALIA MELON

2 KIWIFRUIT

3-4 MINT SPRIGS

I TABLESPOON LEMON JUICE

I TABLESPOON SUGAR

*A refreshing taste of high summer, served with garden
or wild flowers and fern fronds.*

Cut the melon in half around the 'equator', and discard the seeds. Spoon out the flesh into a bowl, keeping the melon halves to use as containers. Cut the melon flesh into bite-sized pieces. Peel the kiwifruit, cut into bite-sized pieces and add to the melon.

Keeping the 2 best sprigs for decoration, chop the remaining mint leaves finely and put in a bowl. Add the lemon juice and sugar, stirring until the sugar has dissolved. Pour this mixture over the fruit and stir gently.

Pile the fruit and juice into the melon halves, which may be supported in glass dishes or served on individual plates decorated with ferns and garden flowers. Serve chilled.

Serves 2

Baked Stuffed Pears
with Almonds

2 LARGE PEARS, PEELED,
HALVED AND CORED

I TABLESPOON GROUND
ALMONDS

2 TABLESPOONS COTTAGE
CHEESE

I TABLESPOON AMARETTO

I EGG WHITE

50 G (2 OZ) CASTER SUGAR

25 G (I OZ) FLAKED ALMONDS

Place the pears, cored side up, in a 22 x 14 cm (8½ x 5½ inch) ovenproof dish. Put the ground almonds, cottage cheese and Amaretto in a bowl and mix well.

In a grease-free bowl, whisk the egg white until stiff, then gradually add the caster sugar and whisk again until the meringue is firm and glossy. Fold in the almond mixture, then spoon the meringue topping over the pears in the dish, piling it up as much as possible. Sprinkle the flaked almonds over the top.

Bake in a preheated oven, 200°C (400°F), Gas Mark 6, for 20 minutes, or until the pears are tender and the topping is golden brown. Serve at once.

Serves 4

Wine Jellied Summer Fruits

This is impressive, fat-free and very easy to make. All it takes is a little patience, while the jelly layers set, and you can stun your friends with an exotic-looking dessert that is as easy as pie – no, easier.

Put the jelly cubes in a heatproof bowl. Add the boiling water, then leave in a warm place to melt – you can speed up the process by heating briefly in a microwave oven, if you wish. When the jelly has melted into the water, stir well and add the red wine. Mix well, then pour a little of this liquid into a rectangular terrine or loaf tin to a depth of no more than 1 cm (½ inch). Allow to set in the refrigerator while preparing the fruit.

If the strawberries are large, cut them in half, then hull and rinse all the fruit. Put a layer of one sort of fruit in the terrine, over the jelly, and pour more jelly over to cover the fruit by no more than half – any more and it will float. Return the terrine to the refrigerator to set, and place the remaining jelly in a warm place so that it remains liquid. Continue adding layers in this way. I usually make at least 3 layers of different fruits, allowing the jelly to set between each. Finish with a layer of jelly and leave to set fully.

When you are ready to serve, dip the terrine in warm water for a moment before sliding a knife around the edge to loosen the jelly. Turn out on to a large platter, decorate with any remaining fruit and serve.

Serves 6

142 G (5 OZ) TABLET STRAWBERRY OR RASPBERRY JELLY, BROKEN INTO SQUARES
300 ML (½ PINT) BOILING WATER
300 ML (½ PINT) RED WINE
500 G (1 LB) MIXED RED FRUITS (STRAWBERRIES, RASPBERRIES, REDCURRANTS, TAY BERRIES)

Lower Fat
Raspberry Cheesecake

BASE

175 G (6 OZ) DIGESTIVE
BISCUITS (PREFERABLY A
LOW-SUGAR VARIETY)

75 G (3 OZ) LIGHT MARGARINE

FILLING

11 G (½ OZ) SACHET
POWDERED GELATINE

2 TABLESPOONS WATER

175 G (6 OZ) LOW-FAT
CREAM CHEESE

25 G (1 OZ) CASTER SUGAR

150 ML (¼ PINT) LOW-FAT
RASPBERRY YOGURT

250 G (8 OZ) RASPBERRIES,
THAWED IF FROZEN

150 ML (¼ PINT) LOW-FAT
WHIPPING CREAM

Many people enjoy puddings, but feel guilty about eating them, having been brainwashed into thinking they should be as thin as fashion models. This pudding was developed by my friend Anne Stirk for these unfortunate folk, being a gesture in their direction, and in the hope of drawing them back into the fold occupied by we larger, happier people.

Make the base. Melt the light margarine in a small pan over gentle heat – if it gets too hot it will separate. Crumb the biscuits finely in a food processor, or place in a strong polythene bag and crush with a rolling pin. Mix with the melted margarine and press on to the base of an 18 cm (7 inch) round spring-form tin. Smooth the surface, and set aside to set in the refrigerator.

Make the filling. Sprinkle the gelatine on to the measured water in a small heatproof bowl. Leave until spongy, then set the bowl over a saucepan of simmering water until the gelatine has dissolved. Cool it rapidly by pouring it into another bowl.

Mix the cream cheese with the sugar and yogurt in a mixing bowl, then stir in the cooled gelatine. Purée the raspberries in a blender or food processor, then rub them through a sieve to remove the seeds. Whip the low-fat cream in a bowl until thick. Fold the raspberry purée into the cream cheese mixture, then fold in the cream.

Pour the filling over the biscuit base and refrigerate until set.

Serves 4-6

Hot Fruit Compote

Warm up a winter's evening with this comforting pudding.
Greek yogurt makes an excellent accompaniment.

Combine the raisins, apricots and orange juice in a saucepan. Simmer for about 10-12 minutes until the apricots are tender and the raisins have swelled. Remove the pan from the heat.

Peel the oranges, removing as much pith as possible. Using a serrated knife, cut into neat segments, working over the pan to catch the juice. Add the orange segments and banana slices to the pan and stir gently. Return the pan to the heat and warm through for a few minutes. Tip into a heated serving bowl, stir in the brandy and serve.

Serves 6

I TABLESPOON RAISINS

125 G (4 OZ) DRIED APRICOTS

300 ML (½ PINT) FRESHLY
SQUEEZED ORANGE JUICE

3 ORANGES

2 BANANAS, SLICED

3-4 TABLESPOONS BRANDY

Rose Fruit Salad

Combine the jelly, honey, mint and measured water in a saucepan. Bring to the boil, then remove from the heat and leave to infuse for about 10 minutes. Remove the mint with a slotted spoon.

Stir the rosewater into the redcurrant jelly mixture and pour it into a serving bowl. Prepare the fruit according to the type used and cut into bite-sized pieces. Add the fruit while the liquid is still warm, so that the flavours blend. Chill the fruit salad in the refrigerator. Just before serving, decorate with the mint sprigs and rose petals.

Serves 4

I TABLESPOON REDCURRANT
JELLY

2 TABLESPOONS CLEAR HONEY

2 MINT SPRIGS

600 ML (I PINT) WATER

I TEASPOON CONCENTRATED
ROSEWATER

750G (I½ LB) FRESH FRUIT
(PEACHES OR NECTARINES
AND CHERRIES)

TO DECORATE

MINT SPRIGS

ROSE PETALS

Sunshine Strawberry Ring

200 G (7 OZ) SELF-RAISING
FLOUR

25 G (1 OZ) CORNFLOUR

¼ TEASPOON SALT

25 G (1 OZ) SUGAR, PLUS
EXTRA, FOR SPRINKLING

25 G (1 OZ) BUTTER

150 ML (¼ PINT) MILK

500 G (1 LB) STRAWBERRIES,
HULLED

If you grow (or even pick) your own strawberries, a glut often means you want to find new ways of using them. Here is one I remember from my childhood. It was served on a big flat platter covered with strawberry leaves, which my Granny said were symbols of a duke or duchess. It is called sunshine not just because the fresh strawberries are a height of summer fruit, but because the slashed dough looks, when baked golden brown, like a stylized sun.

Lightly grease a baking sheet. Mix the flour, cornflour, salt and sugar in a large bowl. Rub in the butter until the mixture resembles fine breadcrumbs. Reserve about 1 tablespoon of milk for glazing; pour the rest into the crumbed mixture and mix to a soft dough. Different flours absorb different amounts of liquid, so the quantity of milk is approximate; aim for a dough that is soft enough to roll out easily on a lightly floured surface.

Roll out the dough to a 50 x 20 cm (20 x 8 inch) rectangle. Roll up from the longest side, as when making a Swiss roll, then bring the ends of the roll together to form a ring. Dampen the ends with a little water and tuck one inside the other to make a neat circle. Using a sharp knife, make slashes around the circle, about 2.5 cm (1 inch) apart, each time cutting about halfway through the dough ring.

Put the ring on the baking sheet. Using your hands, gently ease the circle outwards to make it slightly bigger. This will open out the cuts and give a jagged edge resembling rays of sunshine. Brush with the reserved milk and sprinkle the sugar over the top.

Bake in a preheated oven, 220°C (425°F), Gas Mark 7, for 15 minutes until golden and cooked through; the ring should sound hollow when tapped, like a loaf of bread. Cool on a wire rack.

Just before serving, pile the strawberries in the centre of the ring, adding a few extra around the sides, if liked.

Serves 8

Champagne Jelly
with Strawberries

The strawberry in each glass seems to be suspended in the wine by magic.

Heat the wine gently in a pan. As soon as it approaches simmering point remove it from the heat and sprinkle the gelatine over the top. Stir until all the gelatine crystals have dissolved. Half fill 6 tall long-stemmed glasses with the liquid; refrigerate until the jelly has set. Keep the remaining jelly mixture in a warm place so that it remains liquid.

Place a strawberry on top of the jelly in each glass. Pour over just enough jelly to hold the strawberry in place (about halfway up the fruit), and return the glasses to the refrigerator until the jelly has set. Finally, top up each glass with the remaining liquid jelly; refrigerate until set.

1.2 LITRES (2 PINTS) CHAMPAGNE OR SPARKLING WINE

2 X 11 G (½ OZ) SACHETS POWDERED GELATINE

6 PERFECT STRAWBERRIES, WITH THE GREEN CALYX ATTACHED

Purple Hearts

Line 8 small heart-shaped moulds or ramekins with clingfilm, which will make it easy to turn out when set. Sprinkle the jelly crystals over the boiling water in a heatproof bowl, stir well and leave for a few minutes to dissolve. Hull the strawberries and cut into pieces about the same size as the blackcurrants. Stir the liqueur into the jelly and add all the fruit. Spoon a mixture of fruit and jelly into each mould, easing the mixture into any corners. Use a generous amount of fruit to liquid; you will probably have some of the jelly left over, but should use all the fruit. Chill until set, then turn out on to plates to serve. Decorate with cream and a sliced strawberry.

Serves 8

95 G (3½ OZ) PACKET BLACK-CURRANT JELLY CRYSTALS

450 ML (¾ PINT) BOILING WATER

250 G (8 OZ) STRAWBERRIES

250 G (8 OZ) BLACKCURRANTS, THAWED IF FROZEN

3 TABLESPOONS CRÈME DE CASSIS

TO DECORATE

WHIPPED CREAM

SLICED STRAWBERRIES

Exotic Fruit Baskets

4 LARGE SHEETS OF FILO
PASTRY, THAWED IF FROZEN
50 G (2 OZ) BUTTER, MELTED
A SELECTION OF FRESH FRUIT,
SUCH AS CARAMBOLA (STAR
FRUIT), STRAWBERRIES,
PAPAYA AND MANGO,
PREPARED ACCORDING TO
TYPE AND CUT INTO
BITE-SIZED PIECES
CONFECTIONERS' CUSTARD
125 G (4 OZ) BUTTER
125 G (4 OZ) PLAIN FLOUR
125 G (4 OZ) CASTER SUGAR
4 EGG YOLKS
½ TEASPOON VANILLA ESSENCE
600 ML (1 PINT) MILK

You will need 6 x 500 g (1 lb) clean jam jars or similar heatproof containers to make the bases for the baskets, plus some foil.

To make the baskets, invert the jars on a large baking sheet, spacing them well apart. Fit a piece of foil over each jar to come at least halfway down the sides. Keeping all the filo sheets together, mark the top sheet into 6 squares, then cut through all the layers simultaneously to give 24 squares in all. Drape 1 small square over each jar, brush with a little melted butter, then add a second square, giving the jar a quarter turn so that the filo corners fall down in different places. Brush with more melted butter. Repeat with the remaining filo squares, brushing each layer with the melted butter, until each of the 6 jars have 4 filo squares.

Bake in a preheated oven, 190°C (375°F), Gas Mark 5, for 5-8 minutes, until all the pastry layers are crisp and golden. Remove the baking sheet from the oven and allow the pastry baskets to cool on the jars for 5 minutes. Slide the fragile baskets very carefully off the foil-covered jars, and cool them on a wire rack.

Make the confectioners' custard. Melt the butter in a saucepan. Add the flour and sugar and mix well, stirring constantly over a very gentle heat. Gradually add the egg yolks, vanilla essence and milk, stirring all the time until the mixture approaches simmering point and thickens to a custard. Cover closely and allow to cool.

Just before serving, spoon a little of the confectioners' custard into each filo basket. Pile the prepared fruit on top and serve.

Serves 6

Right: *Exotic Fruit Baskets*

Pears with Almonds
in Hot Chocolate Sauce

175 G (6 OZ) CASTER SUGAR

350 ML (12 FL OZ) WATER (OR

A MIXTURE OF WATER AND

WHITE WINE)

2 TABLESPOONS LEMON JUICE,

PLUS EXTRA FOR BRUSHING

PEARS, IF REQUIRED

1 TEASPOON VANILLA ESSENCE

4 PEARS

50 G (2 OZ) FLAKED ALMONDS,

TOASTED, TO DECORATE

HOT CHOCOLATE SAUCE

150 ML (¼ PINT) SINGLE

CREAM

1 TABLESPOON CASTER SUGAR

175 G (6 OZ) GOOD PLAIN

CHOCOLATE, BROKEN INTO

SQUARES

Escoffier created the original recipe, calling it Poires Belle Hélène.
This is a simplified version.

Put the sugar and water (or wine mixture) in a saucepan large enough to hold all the pears upright. Add the lemon juice and vanilla essence and heat gently until the sugar has dissolved. Bring to the boil, lower the heat and simmer the syrup gently while you prepare the pears.

Using a potato peeler, peel the pears thinly, leaving any stalks on the fruit. Carefully scoop out the cores, leaving a flat base so that the pears will stand up. If the pears start to discolour, brush them with the extra lemon juice.

Stand the pears upright in the saucepan of syrup. Tent a piece of crumpled greaseproof paper or nonstick baking paper over the pan so that the parts of the pears not immersed in the liquid will cook in the steam. Simmer for 20-30 minutes or until the pears are tender and look almost translucent. Lift out carefully, drain and cool. Reserve the syrup for use in another recipe.

Make the sauce. Combine the cream and sugar in a small saucepan. Bring to the boil, stirring to dissolve all the sugar. Take the pan off the heat and add the chocolate. Stir until it has melted into the sauce.

To serve, stand each pear upright on a plate, pour some of the sauce over, and sprinkle with the toasted almonds. Serve any remaining sauce separately.

Serves 4

Baked Orange & Apricot
Cheesecake

Standard breakfast muesli is used for the base of this cheesecake, which is of the traditional baked variety. Honey, apricots and oranges combine to make a sweet that is nice and not too naughty.

Line and grease an 18 cm (7 inch) round loose-bottomed cake tin. Simmer the dried apricots in the orange juice in a saucepan for about 10 minutes or until tender. Meanwhile, melt the butter with 1 tablespoon of the honey in a small saucepan; mix in the muesli until well coated. Press the mixture on to the base of the prepared cake tin, and set aside until firm.

Cool the apricot mixture slightly, then purée the apricots with the juice in a blender or food processor. Spread about a third of the purée over the muesli base. Put the rest of the purée in a small bowl. Add the remaining honey and fromage frais and mix well, then pour the mixture carefully over the apricot purée in the tin.

Bake in a preheated oven, 190°C (375°F), Gas Mark 5, for 35-40 minutes, or until the cheesecake comes away from the sides of the tin. Cool in the tin for at least 5 minutes before transferring the cheesecake to a serving plate.

Serves 4-6

175 G (6 OZ) DRIED APRICOTS
175 ML (6 FL OZ) FRESHLY
SQUEEZED ORANGE JUICE
75 G (3 OZ) BUTTER
2 TABLESPOONS CLEAR HONEY
250 G (8 OZ) MUESLI
500 G (1 LB) FROMAGE FRAIS

Summer Pudding

750 G (1½ LB) SOFT FRUITS,
PREFERABLY THREE
DIFFERENT VARIETIES,
PREPARED ACCORDING
TO TYPE
I TABLESPOON WATER
125 G (4 OZ) CASTER SUGAR
ABOUT 250 G (8 OZ) SLICED
WHITE BREAD, CRUSTS
REMOVED

As this is an all-time favourite, it is worth making plenty of puddings in late summer, when the red fruits such as raspberries, redcurrants, strawberries and tay berries are in season.

Line a 900 ml (1½ pint) pudding basin with clingfilm, leaving a generous overlap. This is not necessary, but it will make the pudding easier to turn out. Put the prepared fruits in a saucepan. Add the measured water and sugar. Heat gently until the sugar has dissolved. Simmer for 5 minutes or less, until the juices have begun to run from the fruit but before it has become a pulp.

Use most of the bread slices to line the pudding basin, cutting and filling so that there are no gaps. Tip the fruit into the basin, filling it almost to the top. Reserve some of the juice. Cover the fruit with more bread, then place a plate on top and add a light weight.

Chill for several hours or overnight in the refrigerator. To serve, invert the pudding in a shallow bowl or lipped plate. Use the reserved juice to moisten any parts of the bread where the dark red juice has failed to penetrate. Serve at once, with cream, if liked.

Serves 6

Variation

Don't think you can only make this in late summer – it works well with frozen fruit, or you can create an autumn version with dried fruits such as figs and apricots. Some shops sell a mixture of dried fruits, which make an excellent pudding. You will need less sugar than when using berry fruit, as the natural sugars in the fruit are concentrated during the drying process. You need less fruit, too – about 500 g (1 lb) – but you should increase the amount of water to 150 ml (¼ pint). Adding 1 teaspoon ground cinnamon improves the flavour.

Right: *Summer Pudding*

Upside Down Tart
with Three Fruits

50 G (2 OZ) BROWN SUGAR

3 ORANGES, PEELED AND
SEGMENTED

2 PEARS, PEELED AND SLICED

2 APPLES, PEELED AND SLICED

300 G (10 OZ) SELF-RAISING
FLOUR

175 G (6 OZ) BUTTER, PLUS
EXTRA FOR GREASING

50 G (2 OZ) GRANULATED
SUGAR

PINCH OF SALT

I EGG, BEATEN

When you have finished giggling at the picture conjured up by this recipe, it is worth remembering that this is a very easy and versatile pudding which can be rustled up fairly quickly. You can vary the combination of fruits according to what is available. Remember to take more care with the appearance of the base than the top, since this will be on view when the tart is inverted for serving.

Grease a 20 cm (8 inch) round flan dish or cake tin. Don't use a loose-bottomed tin or the juice may leak out during baking. Sprinkle the brown sugar on the base of the dish or tin, then place the fruit on top, arranging the segments and slices in concentric circles. Keep the fruit as level as possible.

Make a rich pastry: place the flour, butter, granulated sugar and salt in a food processor and process until the mixture resembles fine breadcrumbs. Alternatively, mix the dry ingredients in a bowl, cut in the butter and rub it into the mixture. If using the processor, add the egg through the feeder tube, with the motor running; this should be just enough to bring the mixture together into a ball. If you are working by hand, you will probably need to add a little cold water with the egg in order to bring the dough together; use as little water as possible. This results in a very soft dough, which can be pressed out by hand to a circle big enough to cover the fruit layer in the dish.

Cover the fruit with the pastry, tuck any edges in, and press down lightly. Bake the tart in a preheated oven, 200°C (400°F), Gas Mark 6, for 30 minutes or until the pastry is cooked and golden. Cool in the tin for 5 minutes before inverting it on a serving plate. The tart may be served hot or cold, but is at its best when just warm.

Serves 6

Hot Baked Nectarines

You can make this with peaches if you prefer, but I find that the skins are often rather tough, and it can take a while to peel them. Smooth-skinned nectarines can be baked and eaten with the peel left on, so they keep their shape better and still taste good. This recipe can easily be adapted to serve any number of guests.

Put the cream cheese in a bowl, add the sugar, then beat together until smooth. Work in the ground almonds to make a fairly stiff paste, then stuff both halves of each fruit, pressing the paste down into the cavity left by the stone.

Arrange the nectarines in a shallow baking dish. Smooth the surface of each with a fork and sprinkle with flaked almonds. Bake in a preheated oven, 200°C (400°F), Gas Mark 6, for 6-10 minutes or until the fruit is hot and the almonds are toasted. Serve hot with cream or yogurt.

PER PERSON:

1 TABLESPOON CREAM CHEESE

½ TABLESPOON CASTER SUGAR

½ TABLESPOON GROUND ALMONDS

1 NECTARINE, HALVED AND STONED

FLAKED ALMONDS, TO DECORATE

Baked Peaches

Cut the peaches in half and place cut side down in a shallow ovenproof dish. Sprinkle with the sugar and pour the wine over the top. Bake in a preheated oven, 180°C (350°F), Gas Mark 4, for 30 minutes or until tender.

Using a slotted spoon, transfer the peaches to a shallow serving dish; pour the cooking juices into a small pan. In a cup, mix the arrowroot with a little water to form a smooth paste. Add the arrowroot mixture to the juices in the pan. Heat gently, stirring constantly, until the liquid thickens and clears. Allow to bubble for only a few seconds, then pour the mixture over the peach halves; as it cools, it will form a delicious thick glaze.

Serves 4

4 RIPE PEACHES, PEELED AND STONED

25 G (1 OZ) CASTER SUGAR

200 ML (7 FL OZ) SWEET WHITE WINE

2 TEASPOONS ARROWROOT

Billy's Amazing
Curried Fruit Salad

432 G (15 OZ) CAN PINEAPPLE

CHUNKS IN NATURAL JUICE

50 G (2 OZ) DRIED APRICOTS

I TABLESPOON CLEAR HONEY

¼ TEASPOON TURMERIC

¼ TEASPOON GROUND GINGER

¼ TEASPOON GROUND CUMIN

½ STICK CINNAMON

3 TABLESPOONS WATER

2 BANANAS, SLICED

NATURAL YOGURT, TO SERVE

The amazing is because, until I tried this, I would never have believed that a curried fruit salad could be anything other than a nightmare. Billy was a student friend of my daughter's who forcefully insisted this pudding was good, and that I should try it. I did, and so should you.

Drain the pineapple chunks, reserving the juice in a pan. Add the apricots, honey, turmeric, ginger, cumin, cinnamon and measured water to the pan. Simmer gently for 5 minutes. Remove the cinnamon stick, add the pineapple chunks and bananas and mix gently. Allow the mixture to heat through, adding a little more water if necessary. Pour into a serving dish and serve warm, adding a spoonful of natural yogurt to each portion.

Serves 4

Gooseberry and
Elderflower Fool

375 G (12 OZ) GOOSEBERRIES,

THAWED IF FROZEN

125 G (4 OZ) CASTER SUGAR

I TABLESPOON WATER

3 HEADS OF ELDERFLOWERS

OR I TABLESPOON

ELDERFLOWER CORDIAL

250 G (8 OZ) GREEK YOGURT

If using fresh gooseberries, top and tail them, then put in a pan with the sugar and measured water. It should not be necessary to add water to frozen fruit. Simmer fresh gooseberries for 10 minutes, frozen fruit for 5 minutes or until soft. If using elderflower cordial, stir it in at the end of the cooking time; if using fresh flower heads, add to the pan about halfway through cooking.

When the gooseberries are cooked, remove from the heat and cool. Remove the flower heads, if used. Purée the gooseberries (with the cooking liquid) by pressing them through a sieve into a bowl. Stir in the yogurt fairly roughly, to create a ripple effect. Pile into stemmed glass dishes and chill before serving.

Serves 4

Rhubarb Brown Betty

East Ardsley, near Leeds, has been the home of rhubarb growers for many generations, and whole trainloads of the tender shoots used to leave there during the season. There is much less rhubarb now, but I still think of it very much as a northern dish, no nonsense and down to earth stuff, associated with someone saying, 'Get it down yer, it'll do you good'.

Put the rhubarb in a saucepan with the sultanas, measured water and sugar. Bring to the boil over a gentle heat, stirring from time to time to dissolve the sugar. Simmer for a few minutes, until the rhubarb is just tender but has not lost its shape, then drain and set aside.

Melt the butter in a clean saucepan, and use some of it to grease a deep oven-proof dish. In a bowl, mix the breadcrumbs, crushed biscuits, brown sugar and cinnamon. Stir a few drops of lime oil into the remaining melted butter, if liked, then add this to the dry ingredients and mix well.

Layer a third of the cooked rhubarb in the base of the dish. Spread a third of the crumb mixture on top. Repeat the layers twice more until all the ingredients have been used.

Bake in a preheated oven, 190°C (375°F), Gas Mark 5, for 30 minutes, until the topping is golden brown and crisp. Serve warm, with cream or yogurt, if liked.

Serves 6

750 G (1½ LB) RHUBARB, TRIMMED AND CUT INTO CHUNKS

125 G (4 OZ) SULTANAS

3 TABLESPOONS WATER

125 G (4 OZ) GRANULATED SUGAR

200 G (7 OZ) BUTTER

125 G (4 OZ) FRESH BROWN BREADCRUMBS

175 G (6 OZ) DIGESTIVE BISCUITS, CRUSHED

125 G (4 OZ) SOFT DARK BROWN SUGAR

1 TEASPOON GROUND CINNAMON

FEW DROPS OF LIME OIL (OPTIONAL)

Banana Turnovers

1 TABLESPOON LEMON JUICE

4 BANANAS

25 G (1 OZ) BUTTER, MELTED

25 G (1 OZ) SOFT DARK
BROWN SUGAR

375 G (12 OZ) PUFF PASTRY,
THAWED IF FROZEN

1 EGG, BEATEN

25 G (1 OZ) ICING SUGAR

Put the lemon juice in a shallow bowl. Peel the bananas, then slice them quite thinly into the bowl. Turn to coat all the slices in the lemon juice. Add the melted butter and brown sugar; mix gently.

Roll out the pastry to a thickness of 3 mm (⅛ inch) and cut out 8 circles with a 10 cm (4 inch) pastry cutter. Using the rolling pin, flatten the circles slightly to create oval shapes.

Divide the banana mixture between the ovals, and brush around the edges with a little water. Fold each oval in half and seal well, pressing the edges with the tines of a fork to make a good seal. Place the turnovers on a baking sheet and glaze with the beaten egg. Any remaining pastry can be cut into shapes and used to decorate the turnovers, if liked.

Bake in a preheated oven, 220°C (425°F), Gas Mark 7, for 10 minutes, then flip the turnovers over and bake for 5 minutes more. Remove the baking sheet from the oven, sift the icing sugar over the turnovers, then return them to the oven for a further 2 minutes until the sugar coating is golden brown. Serve hot with cream or custard.

Serves 4

Braised Pears
with Honey Saffron Custard

Saffron consists of the stamens of a type of crocus, and although this spice is very expensive, you only need a pinch to transform the colour and flavour of many dishes. Use whole saffron threads if possible, crushing them in a mortar and pestle before use.

Put the pear halves in a casserole, pour over the ginger ale, perry or cider and sprinkle the sugar on top. Cover with a lid or foil. Bake in a preheated oven, 190°C (375°F), Gas Mark 5, for 30 minutes, stirring once halfway through the cooking time.

Meanwhile, make the custard. Beat the egg yolks in a bowl. Put the honey, milk and saffron in a large saucepan and warm gently until the mixture approaches boiling point. It is worth doing this slowly in order to extract the maximum flavour and colour from the saffron.

Pour the hot milk on to the beaten egg yolks in a slow steady stream, stirring all the time, then return this mixture to the rinsed-out pan. Heat gently again, stirring all the time until the custard thickens sufficiently to coat the back of a wooden spoon. Pour into a serving dish or jug and allow to cool to lukewarm.

Spoon the pears into individual bowls, ladle a little of the cooking juices over each portion, and serve at once, with the custard.

Serves 4

4 FIRM PEARS (PREFERABLY CONFERENCE), PEELED, HALVED AND CORED

4 TABLESPOONS GINGER ALE, PERRY OR CIDER

2 TABLESPOONS SOFT DARK BROWN SUGAR

HONEY SAFFRON CUSTARD

3 EGG YOLKS

1 TABLESPOON CLEAR HONEY

300 ML (½ PINT) MILK

¼ TEASPOON SAFFRON THREADS OR POWDERED SAFFRON

Ices & Sorbets

Gin & Lavender Ice Cream
with Lavender Biscuits

This is sensational for a late summer dinner, when the evening scents from the garden are matched by the smell and smooth taste of the pudding.

Put the lavender flowers in a small bowl. Warm the gin to blood heat and pour over the lavender. Cover and leave in a warm place to infuse for at least 1 hour, by which time the gin will have absorbed the lavender flavour.

Strain the lavender gin through a sieve placed over a measuring jug, pressing the flowers with the back of a spoon to extract maximum flavour. You require 45 ml (1½ fl oz) of liquid, so add more plain gin if necessary.

Heat the honey in a small pan to just below boiling point. Whisk the egg yolks in a bowl until pale and fluffy. Whisking constantly, pour the honey over the egg yolks in a thin steady stream. Continue to whisk until the mixture has begun to cool and almost doubled in volume. Stir in the flavoured gin.

Whip the cream in a bowl until soft peaks form. In a grease-free bowl, whisk the egg whites until stiff. Fold the cream into the egg yolk mixture, then add the beaten egg whites. Put the mixture in a suitable container for freezing; leave in the freezer for 6 hours or overnight before serving.

To make the lavender biscuits, line 2-3 baking sheets with nonstick baking paper. Cream the butter and sugar in a bowl, then add the beaten egg. Stir in the flour and lavender flowers. Drop teaspoons of the mixture, spaced well apart, on the baking sheets. Bake in batches in a preheated oven, 180°C (350°F), Gas Mark 4, for 15 minutes or until golden at the edges. The biscuits will feel soft, but will crisp as they cool. Leave on the sheets for a few minutes, then transfer to wire racks to cool. Serve scoops of ice cream with the biscuits.

Serves 4

1 TABLESPOON DRIED
LAVENDER FLOWERS
5 TABLESPOONS GIN
125 ML (4 FL OZ) CLEAR
HONEY
4 EGG YOLKS
300 ML (½ PINT) DOUBLE
CREAM
2 EGG WHITES
LAVENDER BISCUITS
250 G (8 OZ) UNSALTED OR
LIGHTLY SALTED BUTTER
125 G (4 OZ) CASTER SUGAR
1 EGG, BEATEN
175 G (6 OZ) SELF-RAISING
FLOUR
1 TABLESPOON DRIED
LAVENDER FLOWERS,
CRUMBLED

Left: *Gin & Lavender Ice Cream*

Basic Vanilla Ice Cream

300 ML (½ PINT) MILK

3 EGG YOLKS

75 G (3 OZ) CASTER SUGAR

300 ML (½ PINT) DOUBLE
CREAM

1 TEASPOON VANILLA ESSENCE

Once you have mastered this recipe, you will find there are many delicious variations. The flavourings for the ice cream itself can be altered, as can the sauce that goes with it or the biscuit accompaniments.

Heat the milk gently in a pan. In a bowl, whisk the egg yolks and sugar together until pale and fluffy and the whisk leaves a trail when lifted. Pour the milk on to the egg mixture, whisking all the time, then return it to a clean pan. Heat gently, stirring constantly, to make a thin custard. The mixture must not boil, or it will curdle. When the custard has thickened sufficiently to coat the back of a wooden spoon, pour it into a large bowl and cool – 30 minutes in the refrigerator should be sufficient.

Whip the cream until it just holds its shape, then fold it into the custard. Flavourings are added at this stage; for vanilla, add the vanilla essence, stirring well to distribute the flavour evenly.

Pour the mixture into a suitable container for freezing, cover with a lid or clingfilm and freeze until mushy (when ice crystals form around the sides). This will take about 3 hours.

Remove the ice cream from the freezer and whisk well to break down the ice crystals. Return to the freezer for at least 3 hours, preferably overnight.

Before serving, transfer to the refrigerator for 45 minutes, or allow to stand at room temperature for 15 minutes, so it is soft enough to serve.

Serves 4

Variation

If you want to impart just a hint of vanilla flavouring, as when making an ice cream to serve with exotic fruits, omit the essence and use vanilla sugar. This is made by burying a whole vanilla pod in a jar of caster sugar. The pod will continue to release flavour for over a year, and the flavoured sugar may be used in a variety of puddings and cakes.

Lime & Pine Nut
Ice Cream

As with most nuts, the flavour of pine nuts is intensified by roasting, and as they are expensive, it is worth doing this and doing it carefully. Place them under a hot grill or in a roasting tin in the oven until they are very lightly browned.

Make the basic vanilla ice cream, adding the lime oil with the cream. Freeze until crystals form around the sides of the bowl, then beat well. Stir in the roasted pine nuts; the mixture should be thick enough to prevent the pine nuts from sinking to the bottom. Check halfway through the final freezing time and, if necessary, mix again to distribute the nuts.

Serves 4

I QUANTITY BASIC VANILLA
ICE CREAM (SEE PAGE 68)
½ TEASPOON LIME OIL
75 G (3 OZ) PINE NUTS,
ROASTED AND COOLED

Cheat's Cherry Ripple

Purée the cherry pie filling in a blender or food processor until fairly smooth. Spoon half the purée into a bowl, cover and chill in the refrigerator until required. Stir the remaining purée into the custard in a bowl.

Whip the cream in a separate bowl until it just holds its shape, then fold into the cherry and custard mixture. Mix well and transfer the mixture to a suitable container for freezing. Freeze for about 2½ hours, until almost solid.

Remove the ice cream from the freezer and beat well with a wooden spoon to break up the ice crystals. Add the reserved cherry purée, folding it in lightly to create a ripple effect – do not over-mix.

Return the ice cream to the freezer for several hours, until firm. Transfer to the refrigerator 30 minutes before serving, to soften.

Serves 4-6

375 G (12 OZ) CAN CHERRY
PIE FILLING
500 G (1 LB) CUSTARD
150 ML (¼ PINT) DOUBLE
CREAM

Overleaf, Left: *Emerald Granita, Lemon Sorbet*
Right: *Mango Sorbet*

Lemon Sorbet

125 G (4 OZ) SUGAR

300 ML (½ PINT) WATER

PARED RIND AND JUICE OF

3 LEMONS

1 EGG WHITE

Every sorbet starts with a syrup, which is simply a mixture of sugar and water, heated together. Ring the changes by adding any flavour that takes your fancy. As good lemons are now available all year round, this is a refreshing sorbet with which to begin.

Put the sugar, measured water and lemon rind in a saucepan. Heat gently until the sugar has dissolved – do not stir, but shake the pan gently if necessary. When all the sugar has dissolved, bring to the boil, lower the heat and simmer for 10 minutes. Leave to cool completely, then strain the liquid through a fine sieve into a bowl. Stir in the lemon juice. Pour into a suitable container for freezing and freeze for about 3 hours, or until almost solid.

Whisk the egg white in a grease-free bowl until stiff. Remove the semi-frozen lemon mixture from the freezer and beat with a fork or whisk to break down the ice crystals. Fold in the beaten egg white. Return the sorbet to the freezer for 4 hours or overnight until firm. Transfer to the refrigerator 30 minutes before serving, to soften.

Serves 4

Mango Sorbet

565 G (1¼ LB) CAN MANGO

SLICES IN SYRUP

2 TABLESPOONS LEMON JUICE

1 EGG WHITE

This could be described as a cheat's sorbet, as the syrup is provided by the can of fruit. If you like them, try this with lychees, which will give you an aromatic fruit dessert.

Tip the contents of the can into a blender or food processor. Add the lemon juice and process until smooth. Freeze as for Lemon Sorbet (see recipe above), adding the beaten egg white as indicated in the above recipe.

Serves 4

Melon Granita

Cut the melons in half and take out the seeds. Scoop out the flesh into a food processor and purée until smooth. Add the sugar and orange juice and process briefly to mix.

Transfer the purée to a suitable container for freezing. Freeze for 2 hours or until ice crystals form around the edges of the mixture. Beat lightly with a fork to break up the crystals, then return the mixture to the freezer for 1 hour. Beat again. Repeat this process twice more before leaving to freeze until solid.

Transfer the granita to the refrigerator 30 minutes before serving, to soften. Serve in scoops in chilled glass dishes.

Serves 6

2 RIPE GALIA MELONS
175 G (6 OZ) CASTER SUGAR
2 TABLESPOONS FRESHLY
SQUEEZED ORANGE JUICE

Emerald Granita

A good choice for the health-conscious, this is high in vitamin C, low in calories and fat-free. It also sparkles like emeralds when piled in long-stemmed glass serving dishes.

Scoop the flesh from each kiwifruit half, scraping the skins and squeezing the fruit to extract maximum juice. Purée in a blender or food processor. Add the sugar, blend again, add the water and lemon juice and blend until smooth.

Press the purée through a fine sieve placed over a freezerproof bowl, using the back of a wooden spoon to extract maximum liquid from the seed pulp. Cover and freeze for 2 hours or until ice crystals form around the edges. Beat lightly to break up the crystals, then return the mixture to the freezer for 1 more hour. Beat again and freeze for 1 further hour. Mix for a third time. It should be a frozen slush of ice crystals, ready to serve in long-stemmed glasses.

If the granita is not required at once, replace in the freezer until solid, but transfer to the refrigerator 30 minutes before serving, to soften.

Serves 8

12 KIWIFRUIT, CUT IN HALF
200 G (7 OZ) CASTER SUGAR
600 ML (1 PINT) WATER
2½ TABLESPOONS LEMON
JUICE

Chocolate & Cointreau
Ice Cream with Orange Sauce

1 QUANTITY BASIC VANILLA
ICE CREAM (SEE PAGE 68)
125 G (4 OZ) PLAIN
CHOCOLATE, BROKEN INTO
SQUARES
2 TABLESPOONS COINTREAU
ORANGE SAUCE
300 ML (½ PINT) FRESHLY
SQUEEZED ORANGE JUICE
1 TABLESPOON HONEY
5 TEASPOONS ARROWROOT
5 TABLESPOONS WATER

Chocolate and orange are two flavours that seem made for each other, creating a terrific smooth/sharp contrast.

Following the recipe for the basic vanilla ice cream, make the custard and pour it into a bowl. Melt the chocolate in a heatproof bowl over a saucepan of barely simmering water, add the Cointreau and mix until smooth. Stir the mixture into the cooling custard, mixing well, then set aside to cool further. Continue as for the basic ice cream.

About 1 hour before serving, make the orange sauce. Warm the orange juice and honey in a saucepan over a gentle heat and stir until the honey has melted. Mix the arrowroot and water to a smooth paste in a small bowl, then add to the warm juice, stirring all the time. Bring to the boil; the mixture will thicken and start to clear. Simmer for a few seconds only, stirring, then leave to cool to room temperature.

Serve the ice cream in tall glasses, with the sauce poured over the top, or make a pool of the sauce on each dessert plate and heap scoops of ice cream in the centre. Mint leaves make an attractive decoration.

Serves 4

Right: *Chocolate Cointreau Ice Cream*

Rum & Coconut Ice Cream

I QUANTITY BASIC VANILLA
ICE CREAM (SEE PAGE 68)
125 G (4 OZ) CREAMED
COCONUT, CHOPPED
2 TABLESPOONS RUM

Make the basic vanilla ice cream, adding the chopped creamed coconut to the saucepan when warming the milk. Add the rum with the whipped cream, then proceed as in the basic ice cream recipe.

Serves 4

Cashew Nut Ice Cream
with Mango Sauce

125 G (4 OZ) CASHEW NUTS
I QUANTITY BASIC VANILLA
ICE CREAM (SEE PAGE 68)
2 LARGE RIPE MANGOES,
PEELED AND CUBED, OR
397 G (14 OZ) CAN MANGOES
IN NATURAL JUICE

I first ate this on a memorable day in Kenya, at the Norfolk Hotel. The chef wouldn't part with his recipe, so I did my best to reproduce it when I got back home and I must admit it isn't quite as good as his. Perhaps it has something to do with the ripeness of the mangoes, the heat of the surroundings, the company ... perhaps I should go back.

Roast the cashew nuts under a hot grill until lightly browned; set aside to cool. Chop the nuts roughly by hand – a food processor will grind them too finely and you need quite large chunks. Make the basic vanilla ice cream, adding the cashew nuts after breaking down the ice crystals and before the final freezing. To make the mango sauce, purée the cubed fresh mango in a food processor or rub through a sieve into a bowl. If using canned mangoes, add half the juice from the can when puréeing, adding more juice to the purée if necessary to obtain a thick pouring sauce.

Serve the ice cream on individual dessert plates, making a pool of the mango sauce and placing scoops of the ice cream in the centre.

Serves 4

Bailey's Mocha Ice Cream

*This makes a splendid end to a dinner party, rich and smooth
with quite a kick.*

Following the recipe for the basic vanilla ice cream, make the custard and pour
it into a bowl. Melt the chocolate in a heatproof bowl over barely simmering
water. Add the Bailey's and mix until smooth. Stir this mixture into the warm
custard, then set aside to cool. Continue as for the basic ice cream.

Serves 4

I QUANTITY BASIC VANILLA
ICE CREAM (SEE PAGE 68)
125 G (4 OZ) PLAIN
CHOCOLATE, BROKEN INTO
SQUARES
3 TABLESPOONS BAILEY'S
IRISH CREAM LIQUEUR

Apple & Ginger Ice

Put the apples, measured water, sugar, ginger and lemon juice in a pan and
cook over a gentle heat for 10 minutes, or until the apples are very soft. Remove
from the heat, leave to cool slightly, then purée in a blender or food processor
until smooth.

Scrape the purée into a suitable container for freezing and freeze for 2 hours,
until just firm. Beat until smooth, then return the mixture to the freezer for a
further 45 minutes. Repeat this process 3 times before finally freezing the ice
until solid. Serve straight from the freezer, spooned into chilled glasses.

Serves 6-8

I KG (2 LB) COOKING APPLES,
CORED AND CHOPPED
ROUGHLY
I TABLESPOON WATER
125 G (4 OZ) CASTER SUGAR
2.5 CM (I INCH) PIECE OF
FRESH ROOT GINGER, PEELED
AND FINELY CHOPPED
5 TABLESPOONS LEMON JUICE

Brown Bread Ice Cream

75 G (3 OZ) FRESH BROWN
BREADCRUMBS

75 G (3 OZ) DEMERARA SUGAR

2 EGGS, SEPARATED

I TABLESPOON CLEAR HONEY

450 ML (¾ PINT) DOUBLE
CREAM

Mix the breadcrumbs and sugar in a bowl, then spread out on a baking sheet. Toast in a preheated oven, 200°C (400°F), Gas Mark 6, turning until the sugar melts into the breadcrumbs and looks like a dark, crunchy caramel. Cool.

Beat the egg yolks with the honey. Whip the cream until it just holds its shape, and whisk the egg whites until stiff. Fold the cream into the honey and egg yolk mixture, then fold in the egg whites. Stir in the sugared breadcrumbs.

Put in a suitable container for freezing and leave for several hours or overnight until firm. Transfer to the refrigerator 20-30 minutes before serving.

Serves 4

Two Fruit Bombe

750 G (I½ LB) RASPBERRIES

4 TABLESPOONS ORANGE
LIQUEUR OR ORANGE JUICE

4 TABLESPOONS ICING SUGAR

450 ML (¾ PINT) DOUBLE
CREAM

IO SMALL MERINGUE SHELLS,
BROKEN INTO SMALL PIECES

3 RIPE BANANAS

I QUANTITY BASIC VANILLA
ICE CREAM (SEE PAGE 68)

You will need 2 bowls, a 600 ml (1 pint) and a 2.4 litre (4 pint) one, to create the bombe shape. Place half of the raspberries in a bowl, add the liqueur or juice and sugar and stir until the sugar has dissolved. Purée in a blender or food processor, then rub through a sieve to remove the seeds. Whip the cream until it just holds its shape. Mix the meringue pieces with the cream and add the raspberry purée, cutting it into the creamy mixture – don't mix too well.

Oil the larger bowl and line with clingfilm. Add the raspberry mixture. Make a well in the centre by wrapping clingfilm around the oiled outer surface of the small bowl and pressing it into the mixture. Place a weight inside the small bowl to keep it to the required level. Cover and freeze for 3 hours.

Purée the bananas and mix with the vanilla ice cream. Remove the small bowl from the raspberry ice cream centre and remove the clingfilm. Fill the well with the banana ice cream. Cover and return to the freezer for 3 hours or overnight. Unmould the bombe on to a plate and transfer to the refrigerator for 30 minutes before serving.

Serves 8-10

Rhubarb Ice Cream

I invented this for Fred Talbot, This Morning's legendary weatherman. The first sign of spring is often Fred's telling us how far his rhubarb has sprouted, and he often asks for recipes which are not too calorific (bearing in mind that the weather map floats on the water and Fred walks on top). This seemed the least fattening ice cream I could think of. People are often intrigued by the flavour and can't quite place which fruit has been used.

250 G (8 OZ) RHUBARB,
TRIMMED AND CUT INTO
2.5 CM (1 INCH) CHUNKS
125 G (4 OZ) SUGAR
1 TABLESPOON WATER
250 G (8 OZ) GREEK YOGURT
2 EGG WHITES

Put the rhubarb, sugar and measured water in a large saucepan, cover and heat gently to simmering point. Remove the lid and cook gently for 10 minutes, by which time the rhubarb should have disintegrated to a mush. Transfer the contents of the pan to a blender or food processor and process to a smooth purée. Scrape the purée into a large mixing bowl. Refrigerate until cool.

Add the yogurt to the rhubarb purée, mixing well. Whisk the egg whites in a separate, grease-free bowl until stiff, then fold them into the rhubarb mixture. Pour the mixture into a suitable container for freezing.

Freeze the ice cream for several hours or until firm. There is no need to beat the ice cream during the freezing process, but it should be transferred to the refrigerator 20-30 minutes before serving so it is soft enough to be scooped into serving bowls.

Serves 4-6

White Chocolate Ice Cream

150 G (5 OZ) WHITE
CHOCOLATE, BROKEN INTO
SQUARES
½ TEASPOON VANILLA ESSENCE
3 EGG YOLKS
150 ML (¼ PINT) DOUBLE
CREAM
5 EGG WHITES

Melt the white chocolate in a heatproof bowl over hot water. Do not hurry this by stirring, but leave for 15 minutes or more, keeping the water in the pan at below simmering point. As soon as the chocolate has melted, remove from the heat and add the vanilla essence and egg yolks. Mix until well blended.

Whip the cream until thick. Whisk the egg whites in a grease-free bowl until stiff. Fold the cream into the chocolate mixture, then fold in egg whites. Put in a suitable container for freezing and freeze for several hours or overnight until firm. Transfer to the refrigerator 20-30 minutes before serving, to soften.

Serves 4

Baked Alaska

1 LITRE (1¾ PINT) ROUND TUB
OF ICE CREAM
20 CM (8 INCH) ROUND
SPONGE CAKE BASE
2 TABLESPOONS SHERRY OR
ORANGE JUICE
250 G (8 OZ) FRESH OR
DRAINED CANNED FRUIT
3 EGG WHITES
175 G (6 OZ) CASTER SUGAR

Preheat the oven to 230°C (450°F), Gas Mark 8. The ice cream must be kept in the freezer until the last moment, so assemble the rest of the ingredients first. Put the sponge base on an ovenproof dish and moisten with sherry or orange juice. Prepare the fruit.

Whisk the egg whites until very stiff, then gradually whisk in the sugar until thick and glossy. Spread a little less than half the fruit on the sponge base.

Remove the ice cream from the freezer, take it out of the tub in a solid block and place on top of the fruit on the sponge base. Spread the rest of the fruit over the top, and if possible, the sides of the ice cream. Cover this mound with a thick coating of meringue, making sure that the sides of the cake base are covered. Quickly pull the meringue into peaks with the back of a spoon, but make sure that all the ice cream is completely hidden.

Put into the hot oven for 3 minutes, so that the meringue begins to brown at the edges but the ice cream remains frozen. Serve immediately.

Serves 6-8

Christmas Pudding
Ice Cream

If you want a more refreshing finale to Christmas dinner than the usual plum pudding, this is it. Serve it solo – or offer the adults a spoonful of Glacé Fruits in Rum (see below) as an accompaniment.

Line a pudding basin with clingfilm. Put the mixed dried fruit in a bowl and add the brandy and mixed spice. Stir, then leave for at least 1 hour so that the fruit begins to absorb the brandy.

Whip the cream until it just begins to hold its shape, then sift the icing sugar over the top and fold it in. Fold in the soaked fruits, with their liquid, then add the cherries, dates and nuts. Put the mixture in the pudding basin. Cover and freeze for several hours or overnight, until firm.

An hour before serving, turn out on to a serving plate, remove the clingfilm and place in the refrigerator to soften.

Serves 8

300 G (10 OZ) MIXED DRIED FRUIT

4 TABLESPOONS BRANDY

2 TEASPOONS MIXED SPICE

600 ML (1 PINT) DOUBLE CREAM

75 G (3 OZ) ICING SUGAR

125 G (4 OZ) GLACÉ CHERRIES

125 G (4 OZ) CHOPPED DATES

50 G (2 OZ) HAZELNUTS, ROASTED AND CHOPPED

Glacé Fruits in Rum

This colourful mixture keeps well for about a month and is delicious with ice cream, pancakes, or as a filling for baked apples. The combination of fruits is up to you; I use a mixture of glacé papaya, pineapple and kiwifruit, with cherries of various colours.

Chop the fruits into chunks or dice of roughly the same size. Put them into a large clean jar and pour the rum over. Leave to soak for several days, a week if possible, shaking daily.

Makes 250 g (8 oz)

250 G (8 OZ) ASSORTED GLACÉ FRUITS

300 ML (½ PINT) RUM

Chocolate Treats

Spiced Chocolate Gâteau

Chocolate comes originally from Mexico, where the beans were once used as currency, and even then they were so precious that the Aztecs let only the upper classes drink chocolate – a spicy, frothy confection. The combination of chocolate with spices is an ancient and classic one, but instead of the savoury spiced chocolate sauce with turkey that I tasted in Mexico City, you may find the gentler combination with cinnamon in this luscious gâteau more to modern taste.

Line and grease a 23 cm (9 inch) round loose-bottomed cake tin. Combine the egg yolks and caster sugar in a large mixing bowl. Whisk until the mixture is light and fluffy. Stir in the chocolate, cinnamon, grated lemon rind and juice, ground almonds and brandy.

In a separate, grease-free bowl, whisk the egg whites until stiff, then fold them into the chocolate mixture. Mix the breadcrumbs with the baking powder in another bowl, then fold them into the lightened chocolate mixture. Turn into the prepared tin.

Bake in a preheated oven, 160°C (325°F), Gas Mark 3, for 1-1¼ hours or until a skewer inserted into the centre of the cake comes out clean. Cool in the tin for 5-10 minutes before turning the cake out on to a wire rack to cool completely.

To decorate, swirl whipped cream over the top and sides of the gâteau, and then finish with grated chocolate or chocolate leaves.

Serves 6

5 EGGS, SEPARATED

200 G (7 OZ) CASTER SUGAR

4 TABLESPOONS GRATED PLAIN CHOCOLATE

1 TEASPOON GROUND CINNAMON

GRATED RIND AND JUICE OF 1 LEMON

125 G (4 OZ) GROUND ALMONDS

4 TABLESPOONS BRANDY

125 G (4 OZ) DRIED WHOLEMEAL BREADCRUMBS

2 TEASPOONS BAKING POWDER

TO DECORATE

WHIPPED CREAM

GRATED CHOCOLATE OR CHOCOLATE LEAVES

Rich Almond
Chocolate Puddings

40 G (1½ OZ) PLAIN
CHOCOLATE, BROKEN INTO
SQUARES
1 TABLESPOON CASTER SUGAR
1 TABLESPOON ORANGE JUICE,
BRANDY OR LIQUEUR
(PREFERABLY COINTREAU OR
AMARETTO)
1 TABLESPOON DOUBLE CREAM
3 DIGESTIVE BISCUITS,
CRUSHED
1 TABLESPOON GROUND
ALMONDS
COCOA POWDER, FOR SIFTING
2 PERFECT STRAWBERRIES, TO
DECORATE

I often make this in little heart-shaped moulds for Valentine's Day, as I'm married to a chocoholic; but only if he has remembered to buy me flowers first. It's very easy to make, even for someone who isn't accustomed to cooking.

Line 2 small heart-shaped moulds, ramekins or tartlet tins, about 7 cm (3 inches) in diameter, with nonstick baking paper or foil. Melt the chocolate in a heatproof bowl over a saucepan of barely simmering water, then add all the other ingredients except the cocoa powder and strawberries; mix well.

Divide the chocolate mixture between the prepared moulds, pressing it down firmly. Chill in the refrigerator for several hours or overnight.

Turn the puddings out on to individual plates. Sift a little cocoa powder over each and decorate each pudding with a sliced strawberry. Alternatively, serve the puddings on a pool of strawberry sauce or cream. Add some chocolate curls or leaves, if liked.

Serves 2

Pineapple Truffle Loaf

Don't be tempted to use canned pineapple for this; although it will work perfectly well, the flavour will lack the enticing sweet sharpness imparted by the fresh fruit. Save this for a time when there are good ripe pineapples in the shops.

Line 1 x 1 kg (2 lb) or 2 x 500 g (1 lb) loaf tins with nonstick baking paper or foil. Weigh the diced pineapple; put 375 g (12 oz) in a bowl and set the rest aside for decoration. Add the rum and vanilla essence to the bowl of pineapple, stir and set aside for up to 2 hours to allow the flavours to blend and develop. Combine the chocolate, coconut and butter in a heatproof bowl. Place over a saucepan of barely simmering water until the chocolate has melted. Stir until combined. Crumb the ginger biscuits finely in a food processor, or place in a strong polythene bag and crush with a rolling pin.

Stir the biscuit crumbs into the chocolate mixture. Add the pineapple, with the soaking liquid, and stir until thoroughly mixed. Pile the mixture into the lined tin or tins, pressing down lightly. Smooth the surface with a spatula. Chill in the refrigerator for several hours or overnight.

To serve, invert each loaf on to a platter. Decorate with the reserved pineapple chunks, placing them in a neat row down the centre, so that each slice will be topped with a pineapple chunk.

Serves 10

1 MEDIUM TO LARGE PINEAPPLE, TRIMMED AND DICED
4 TABLESPOONS DARK RUM
1 TEASPOON VANILLA ESSENCE
250 G (8 OZ) PLAIN CHOCOLATE, BROKEN INTO SQUARES
175 G (6 OZ) CREAM OF COCONUT, CHOPPED INTO CHUNKS
125 G (4 OZ) BUTTER
200 G (7 OZ) GINGER BISCUITS

Tipsy Chocolate Roulade

175 G (6 OZ) PLAIN
CHOCOLATE, BROKEN INTO
SQUARES
2 TABLESPOONS RUM
5 EGGS, SEPARATED
175 G (6 OZ) CASTER SUGAR,
PLUS EXTRA FOR SPRINKLING
150 ML (¼ PINT) DOUBLE
CREAM
ICING SUGAR, TO DECORATE

This tasty treat can be served simply, with a light dusting of sifted icing sugar, or given the luxury treatment with a decoration of piped whipped cream and chocolate leaves.

Line a 30 x 23 cm (12 x 9 inch) Swiss roll tin with nonstick baking paper. Melt the chocolate with the rum in a heatproof bowl over a pan of barely simmering water. In a separate bowl, combine the egg yolks and caster sugar. Beat with a rotary whisk or hand-held electric mixer until the mixture becomes paler in colour and has increased in volume. Fold in the melted chocolate mixture.

Whisk the egg whites in a grease-free bowl until stiff; fold into the chocolate mixture. Spoon into the prepared tin and level the surface. Bake in a preheated oven, 180°C (350°F), Gas Mark 4, for 20 minutes or until the surface is firm to the touch. Remove from the oven. Cover with a sheet of nonstick baking paper, then a damp tea towel. Leave for several hours or overnight.

When you are ready to assemble the roulade, turn it out on to a sheet of non-stick baking paper or foil which has been thickly sprinkled with caster sugar; peel off the lining paper carefully. Whip the cream in a bowl until thick. Spread over the surface of the sponge, then roll it up, using the nonstick paper as a guide. The roulade may crack, however careful you are, but this does not matter. Use the paper or foil to firm the shape, then transfer the roulade to a serving dish, making sure the join is underneath. Serve in slices.

Serves 6

Right: *Chocolate Roulade*

Chocolate Cherry Roulade

4 EGG WHITES

25 G (1 OZ) COCOA POWDER

200 G (7 OZ) CASTER SUGAR

25 G (1 OZ) DESICCATED

COCONUT

250 G (8 OZ) GREEK YOGURT

375 G (12 OZ) CAN CHERRY

PIE FILLING

This has all the merits of the oft-despised Black Forest Cake, and tastes like the original should (but seldom does).

Line a 30 x 23 cm (12 x 9 inch) Swiss roll tin with nonstick baking paper. Whisk the egg whites in a grease-free bowl until stiff. Sift the cocoa powder into another bowl and stir in the sugar. Add half this mixture to the egg whites and whisk until thick and glossy. Fold in the remaining sugar and cocoa mixture. Pour into the tin and level the surface. Sprinkle the coconut over the top.

Bake in a preheated oven, 190°C (375°F), Gas Mark 5, for 40 minutes. Carefully invert the chocolate sponge on to a sheet of nonstick baking paper and peel off the lining paper. Cover immediately with a damp tea towel and leave to cool.

When cold, spread the sponge with the yogurt and the cherry pie filling. Roll up, using the baking paper as a guide. This will give you a chocolate roll with coconut on the outside. Serve in slices.

Serves 4-6

Chocolate Orange Jelly

This smooth but tangy dessert is popular with young children.

Put the chocolate into a saucepan with the milk. Set over a very low heat to warm just sufficiently to melt the chocolate. Meanwhile, put the jelly squares in a heatproof bowl. Add the orange juice. Place the bowl over a saucepan of simmering water until the jelly has melted into the juice.

Stir the cinnamon into the chocolate and milk mixture, remove from the heat and cool slightly, stirring occasionally. Stir in the liquid jelly, a little at a time, then pour the mixture into a mould or individual serving dishes. Refrigerate until set. The flavour is best if this is served cool rather than cold, so remove the jelly from the refrigerator about 15 minutes before serving.

Serves 4

250 G (8 OZ) PLAIN CHOCOLATE, BROKEN INTO SQUARES
350 ML (12 FL OZ) MILK
142 G (5 OZ) TABLET ORANGE JELLY, BROKEN INTO CUBES
150 ML (¼ PINT) FRESHLY SQUEEZED ORANGE JUICE
½ TEASPOON GROUND CINNAMON

Chocolate Mousse

It is preferable not to make this more than 2-3 hours before serving – if you make it too far in advance you may find that a little liquid separates out at the base of each dish. If preparing the pudding in advance is unavoidable, crumble a digestive biscuit and divide between the dishes before adding the mousse.

Melt the chocolate in a heatproof bowl over a saucepan of barely simmering water. Remove the pan from the heat, leave to cool slightly, then beat in the egg yolks with a wooden spoon. Whisk the egg whites in a grease-free bowl until stiff, then, using a metal spoon, gently fold in the chocolate mixture.

Pour the mixture into 4 little pots or glasses. Refrigerate until set.

Serves 4

125 G (4 OZ) PLAIN CHOCOLATE, BROKEN INTO SQUARES
4 EGGS, SEPARATED

Chocolate & Orange
Pancakes

PANCAKES

90 G (3 OZ) PLAIN FLOUR

15 G (½ OZ) COCOA POWDER

2 EGGS, BEATEN

300 ML (½ PINT) MILK

OIL, FOR FRYING

CASTER SUGAR, FOR

SPRINKLING

FILLING

2 ORANGES, SEGMENTED, OR

270 G (9 OZ) CAN

MANDARIN ORANGES, DRAINED

250 G (8 OZ) GREEK YOGURT

CHOCOLATE SAUCE

125 G (4 OZ) PLAIN

CHOCOLATE, BROKEN INTO

SQUARES

3 TABLESPOONS GOLDEN

SYRUP

25 G (1 OZ) BUTTER, DICED

Make the pancake batter. Sift the flour and cocoa powder into large mixing bowl. Make a well in the centre and add the eggs, with half the milk. Whisk the liquid, gradually incorporating the surrounding flour mixture, to make a smooth batter. Alternatively, make the batter by processing all the batter ingredients together briefly in a blender or food processor. Leave to stand for 30 minutes if possible.

When you are ready to make the pancakes, heat a little oil in a small frying pan or crêpe pan, spoon a little batter into the pan and swirl around to cover the base. Cook until bubbles appear and the surface of the pancake seems dry, then turn, toss or slip over and cook the other side briefly. Slide the cooked pancake on to nonstick baking paper or foil sprinkled with a little caster sugar. Work quickly to make 8 pancakes.

Roll or fold each pancake around a filling of orange segments and a small spoonful of yogurt. Serve 2 pancakes per person, topped with chocolate sauce. To make the chocolate sauce, melt the chocolate, golden syrup and butter together in a heatproof bowl over a saucepan of barely simmering water. As soon as the ingredients have melted, stir until smooth. Pour a little sauce over each portion of pancakes and serve the rest separately.

Chocolate Meringue
Cream Slice

A meringue and almond topping adds interest to this tasty chocolate slice.

Line a 30 x 20 cm (12 x 8 inch) Swiss roll tin with nonstick baking paper. Cream the margarine with half the caster sugar in a mixing bowl, until pale and fluffy. Gradually add the egg yolks, beating well after each addition. Sift the flour, salt, baking powder and cocoa into a separate bowl, mix well, then stir these dry ingredients into the creamed mixture. Add enough of the milk to mix to a soft dropping consistency.

Spread the mixture into the tin, making sure that it fills all the corners. In a grease-free bowl, whisk the egg whites until they are stiff, then gradually whisk in the remaining caster sugar. Spread the meringue over the cake mixture in the tin, and sprinkle the flaked almonds over the top.

Bake in a preheated oven, 180°C (350°F), Gas Mark 4, for 20 minutes. Leave in the tin until cool, then invert the sponge carefully on to a wire rack. Peel off the lining paper. Cut the sponge in half lengthways.

Melt the chocolate in a heatproof bowl over a pan of barely simmering water. In a separate bowl, whip the cream with the icing sugar until soft peaks form. To assemble the slice, put one half of the chocolate sponge on a large serving dish, chocolate side up. Spread with the whipped cream, then place the second portion of cake, chocolate side down, on top. Spoon the melted chocolate into a small piping bag and make a zig-zag design over the top of the slice.

Serves 6

125 G (4 OZ) SOFT MARGARINE

250 G (8 OZ) CASTER SUGAR

2 EGGS, SEPARATED

75 G (3 OZ) PLAIN FLOUR

PINCH OF SALT

2 TEASPOONS BAKING POWDER

4 TABLESPOONS COCOA POWDER

75 ML (3 FL OZ) MILK

125 G (4 OZ) FLAKED ALMONDS

50 G (2 OZ) CHOCOLATE, BROKEN INTO SQUARES

300 ML (½ PINT) WHIPPING CREAM

2 TEASPOONS ICING SUGAR

Chocolate Fruit Towers

375 G (12 OZ) CHOCOLATE,
BROKEN INTO SQUARES
250 G (8 OZ) BERRY FRUIT
(RASPBERRIES, BLUEBERRIES)
250 ML (8 FL OZ) SINGLE
CREAM
GANACHE
250 G (8 OZ) CHOCOLATE,
BROKEN INTO SQUARES
250 ML (8 FL OZ) DOUBLE
CREAM

You can make these little towers of fruit, chocolate and cream from dark or milk chocolate, white chocolate or a mixture, and vary the fruits according to what is available. I first made them with dark chocolate and big juicy blueberries, but used milk chocolate in the ganache filling to give a variety of shades.

Melt the chocolate in a heatproof bowl over a saucepan of barely simmering water. Meanwhile, spread a sheet of nonstick baking paper on a large baking sheet. Using a round or heart-shaped cardboard template with a diameter of about 7 cm (3 inches), draw shapes on the paper – you need at least 2 circles or other shapes per person, and can make smaller chocolate shapes for the tops of the towers.

When the chocolate has melted, use a teaspoon to spread it on to the shapes, working from the centre outwards so as to get a good edge, and spreading the chocolate with the back of the teaspoon to fill the shapes. Put the baking sheet in a cool place (not the refrigerator) until the chocolate has set.

Make the ganache. Put the chocolate in a heatproof bowl. Bring the cream to the boil in a small saucepan, then pour it over the chocolate, stirring all the time. Carry on stirring or whisking until all the chocolate has melted into the cream. The mixture will become fluffy as it cools. This may take a few minutes, so use a hand-held electric mixer if you have one. If you over-beat, the ganache will become too stiff to spread, so stop when it looks like thick cream that will hold its shape.

Spread or pipe the ganache on the chocolate shapes. Sandwich together to build the towers, adding a little fruit to each layer and using more fruit as the topping. Serve on individual plates flooded with cream. Decorate with any remaining fruit.

Serves 6

Triple Chocolate Slice

This frozen dessert will appeal to the chocolate connoisseur, so long as you make it with good quality chocolate. Avoid anything which is described as cooking chocolate or cake covering.

Line a 23 x 12 cm (9 x 5 inch) loaf tin with clingfilm. Put the milk in a saucepan and bring to the boil over a gentle heat. Whisk the egg yolks and sugar in a bowl until pale and creamy. Whisk in the vanilla essence. Add the hot milk, whisking all the time. Return the mixture to a clean pan and heat gently to simmering point, stirring constantly until the custard thickens sufficiently to coat the back of a wooden spoon – do not allow it to boil.

Divide the custard between 3 bowls; allow to cool slightly, then stir each type of chocolate into a different bowl of warm custard until melted and well mixed. Whip the cream in a separate bowl until it is fairly thick and will just hold its shape, then divide the cream between the 3 bowls; mix gently.

Carefully pour each chocolate mixture in turn into the prepared tin, adding the white chocolate layer second, to make three distinct horizontal layers. Put the loaf tin in the freezer for several hours or overnight until firm.

To serve, remove the chocolate slice from the freezer, stand for 5 minutes at room temperature, then ease the dessert out of the tin with the aid of the cling-film lining. Invert on to a serving dish and cut into neat slices.

Serves 8

450 ML (¾ PINT) MILK

6 EGG YOLKS

175 G (6 OZ) CASTER SUGAR

½ TEASPOON VANILLA ESSENCE

125 G (4 OZ) PLAIN CHOCOLATE, BROKEN INTO SQUARES

125 G (4 OZ) MILK CHOCOLATE, BROKEN INTO SQUARES

125 G (4 OZ) WHITE CHOCOLATE, BROKEN INTO SQUARES

450 ML (¾ PINT) DOUBLE CREAM

Overleaf, Left: *White Chocolate Cheesecake*
Right: *Amaretto Truffle Torte*

Amaretto Truffle Torte

500 G (1 LB) PLAIN
CHOCOLATE, BROKEN INTO
SQUARES

5 TABLESPOONS AMARETTO

4 TABLESPOONS GOLDEN
SYRUP

75 G (3 OZ) AMARETTI
BISCUITS

600 ML (1 PINT) DOUBLE
CREAM

2 TABLESPOONS COCOA
POWDER

I consider it a service to humanity to have adapted that fabulous chocolate recipe of Delia Smith's that everyone wanted to make but couldn't get the liquid glucose for. This recipe gives an equally luscious result, but substitutes more readily available golden syrup and uses Amaretto to tie in with the crushed amaretti biscuits. You can make this in a 23 cm (9 inch) round tin, but there is a large amount I find it handier to make two oblong puddings, each of which will serve 4-6, and freeze one. Alternatively, it will keep in the refrigerator for 3 days.

Line 2 x 23 x 12 cm (9 x 5 inch) loaf tins with clingfilm. Melt the chocolate with the Amaretto and syrup in a heatproof bowl over a pan of barely simmering water. Meanwhile, crumb the biscuits finely in a food processor, or place in a strong polythene bag and crush with a rolling pin. Spread the biscuit crumbs on the base of each lined tin.

When the chocolate has melted, stir the mixture until smooth, then pour into a separate bowl to cool. Set aside until the mixture is just warm, and has a smooth texture.

In a separate bowl, whip the cream until it just holds its shape, then fold in the chocolate mixture gently but thoroughly. Spoon this over the crumb layer in both tins, transfer them to the refrigerator and leave for several hours or overnight to set. You can freeze one of the puddings at this stage if you wish.

To serve, invert the pudding(s) on to a serving dish and sift 1 tablespoon of cocoa powder over each. Serve in slices, with cream.

Serves 8-12

White Chocolate Cheesecake

The quantities below make one 25 x 20 cm (10 x 8 inch) or two 20 cm (8 inch) round cheesecakes, each of which would serve about 6. Unless I am entertaining large numbers, I usually make two cheesecakes in deep quiche tins, and freeze one for later. If you choose to do this, you will only need half the quantity of topping ingredients listed, as the frozen cheesecake should be decorated only after thawing.

Grease 1 x 25 x 20 cm (10 x 8 inch) or 2 x 20 cm (8 inch) round cheesecake tins. Make the base. Melt the butter in a saucepan or a jug in the microwave. Finely crumb the biscuits in a food processor, or place in a strong polythene bag and crush with a rolling pin. Mix the butter and crumbs well, then press the mixture on to the base of the greased tin or tins. Chill in the refrigerator until set. Make the filling. Melt the white chocolate in a heatproof bowl over a saucepan of barely simmering water. In a bowl or food processor, cream the softened butter, cream cheese and sugar together. Stir in the melted white chocolate and the beaten eggs. Pour the filling over the crumb base.

Bake in a preheated oven, 160°C (325°F), Gas Mark 3, for 45-60 minutes, until the filling is just set, and browned on top. The filling will rise a little in cooking, especially around the edges, but will fall in the centre as it cools. Leave to cool in the tin. Freeze the spare cheesecake at this stage, if liked. Melt the white chocolate for the topping in a heatproof bowl over a pan of barely simmering water. Stir until smooth, then spread the chocolate in a thin layer over a marble slab or metal baking sheet and leave to set in a cool place. Using a flexible metal palette knife, press down on the chocolate and pull across to form curls. To serve, transfer the cheesecake(s) to a serving dish or plate. Cover with whipped cream and place the white chocolate curls over the top. Finally, dust with a little cocoa powder.

Makes 1 x 25 x 20 cm (10 x 8 inch) cheesecake or 2 x 20 cm (8 inch) cheesecakes

BASE

75 G (3 OZ) BUTTER

300 G (10 OZ) CHOCOLATE-COATED WHOLEMEAL BISCUITS

FILLING

300 G (10 OZ) WHITE CHOCOLATE, BROKEN INTO SQUARES

50 G (2 OZ) BUTTER, SOFTENED

500 G (1 LB) CREAM CHEESE

50 G (2 OZ) CASTER SUGAR

2 EGGS, BEATEN

TOPPING

175 G (6 OZ) WHITE CHOCOLATE, BROKEN INTO SQUARES

450 ML (¾ PINT) DOUBLE CREAM, WHIPPED

COCOA POWDER, FOR DUSTING

Chocolate Fondue

FRESH FRUIT, SUCH AS
BANANAS, APPLES,
STRAWBERRIES, PEARS
AND APPLES
200 G (7 OZ) PLAIN
CHOCOLATE, BROKEN INTO
SQUARES
1 TABLESPOON CLEAR HONEY
2 TABLESPOONS DOUBLE
CREAM
2 TABLESPOONS RUM
(OPTIONAL)

Creamy melted chocolate, with just a hint of rum, makes a delicious dip for chunks of fresh fruit. Use a fondue set if you have one, but don't be deterred from making this dessert if you haven't; a heat-resistant glass saucepan or bowl kept warm over a candle burner works equally well. Set the fondue in the centre of the table and offer forks rather than cocktail sticks for dipping.

Prepare the fruit according to type, cut it into bite-sized chunks and arrange on a large platter or individual plates.

Put the chocolate into a small heatproof bowl with the honey and cream. Set over a saucepan of barely simmering water until the chocolate has melted. Alternatively, heat the mixture gently in a heavy-bottomed fondue pan. Stir in the rum, if using.

Place the bowl or pan over a candle or spirit burner and serve the chocolate fondue at once, with the fruit dippers.

Serves 4-6

Chocolate Terrine

This needs to be rectangular in shape, so that you can cut it in slices to serve. If you do not have a suitable terrine, use a 23 x 12 cm (9 x 5 inch) loaf tin.

Line the terrine or loaf tin with clingfilm, leaving a generous overlap. Put the chocolate into a heatproof bowl. Add half the butter. Place the bowl over a pan of barely simmering water until both chocolate and butter have melted. Stir the mixture until smooth, then remove from the heat.

Whisk the egg yolks with the sugar in another heatproof bowl over hot water until thick, pale and frothy. Gradually whisk in the chocolate mixture. If necessary, soften the remaining pieces of butter. Add them, one at a time, to the chocolate mixture, beating well after each addition. Stir in the orange rind and half the kirsch.

Pour the remaining kirsch into a shallow dish and dilute it with the measured water. To assemble the dessert, spread a thin layer of the chocolate mixture on the base of the lined terrine or tin. Dip the biscuits, one at a time, in the kirsch and water mixture, working swiftly so that they do not disintegrate; arrange a layer of biscuits over the chocolate mixture in the tin. Spread more chocolate mixture on top.

Continue to build up these layers, cutting the dipped biscuits to fit if necessary, until both the chocolate mixture and the biscuits have been used, ending with a layer of biscuits. Level the surface and fold the edges of the clingfilm over. Chill the terrine in the refrigerator for several hours or overnight, until set.

To serve, dip the dish in very hot water for a few seconds to loosen the terrine, then use the film to help you ease it out and invert it on a plate. Serve in slices, with a spoonful of yogurt, if liked.

Serves 6-8

125 G (4 OZ) PLAIN CHOCOLATE, BROKEN INTO SQUARES

250 G (8 OZ) BUTTER, DICED

4 EGG YOLKS

125 G (4 OZ) CASTER SUGAR

FINELY GRATED RIND OF 1 ORANGE

8 TABLESPOONS KIRSCH

4 TABLESPOONS COLD WATER

200 G (7 OZ) SPONGE FINGERS

Profiteroles

300 ML (½ PINT)
DOUBLE CREAM
2 TABLESPOONS BRANDY
250 G (8 OZ) PLAIN
CHOCOLATE, BROKEN INTO
SQUARES
3 TABLESPOONS SINGLE
CREAM
CHOUX PASTRY
150 ML (¼ PINT) WATER
50 G (2 OZ) BUTTER, DICED
60 G (2 OZ) STRONG PLAIN
FLOUR
2 TEASPOONS SUGAR
2 EGGS, BEATEN

If you pile this dessert up into a cone shape and serve it, as I do, on a raised glass cake stand, it can make a stunning tall centrepiece for a sideboard of sweet courses. Don't make too these far in advance of serving.

Start by making the choux pastry. Put the water in a pan with the butter. Have the flour and sugar ready in a bowl so that you can quickly tip the mixture into the pan at the right moment. Warm the butter and water together gently, stirring with a wooden spoon. As soon as the butter has melted, just before the mixture comes to the boil, turn off the heat and tip all the flour and sugar into the pan in a single movement. Whisk vigorously (preferably with a hand-held electric mixer) until the mixture forms a smooth ball that leaves the sides of the pan clean. Beat in the eggs, a little at a time, until the paste is smooth and shiny. To bake, lightly grease a baking sheet. Sprinkle it with a little cold water dripped off the ends of your fingers – this will turn to steam during baking and will help the puffs to rise. Put teaspoons of the pastry, spaced well apart, on the baking sheet. Bake in a preheated oven, 200°C (400°F), Gas Mark 6, for 20-25 minutes until the puffs are crisp and golden. Remove from the oven and make a small cut in the side of each to allow steam to escape. Cool on a wire rack.

To assemble the dessert, whip the cream and brandy together; spoon into a piping bag fitted with a large nozzle. Inserting the nozzle in the slit in the side of each puff, fill with the flavoured cream. Pile the filled puffs up in a conical shape on a serving dish.

Melt the chocolate and cream together in a heatproof bowl over a pan of barely simmering water. As soon as the chocolate has melted, stir to make a smooth sauce. Hold the bowl of chocolate sauce high above the cone of filled puffs and drizzle it over the cone shape, rotating the dish with your other hand so that the sauce spreads evenly. Serve as soon as possible.

Serves 6-8

Hot Chocolate Sauce
for Ice Cream

There is a malicious rumour going the rounds that I was thrown out of a restaurant in Ripon because I ate all the chocolate sauce in a big silver bowl that was intended to serve everybody. This is not true; I did eat all the chocolate sauce (because it was so good, served with an excellent plain ice cream), but they very kindly didn't throw me out that time.

Put the chocolate into a large heatproof bowl with the butter, icing sugar, brandy and orange liqueur. Place the bowl over a saucepan of barely simmering water and leave until the chocolate has melted and warmed through. Stir the mixture thoroughly, then serve at once, ideally with a really good vanilla ice cream.

Since it is important to serve this sauce without delay, I always hand round the chocolate sauce only after the ice cream has been served.

Serves 4

175 G (6 OZ) PLAIN CHOCOLATE, BROKEN INTO SQUARES
25 G (1 OZ) BUTTER
50 G (2 OZ) ICING SUGAR
1 TABLESPOON BRANDY
1 TABLESPOON ORANGE LIQUEUR (COINTREAU OR GRAND MARNIER)

Apple Puddings

Apple Brûlée

I've adapted the recipe for this classic dish – sometimes called Burnt Cream –
to include apples, but it works equally well with pears or a combination of
two fruits, such as apple and orange slices. Whatever fruit you choose, the
secret of success is to make a thick layer of sugar, and finish the
pudding under a very hot grill.

Preheat the grill to its maximum setting. Lightly grease 4 small ramekins – the
dishes must be able to withstand the heat of a hot grill, and should be deep
enough to allow the top of each pudding to brown without further cooking the
base. I use straight-sided ramekins with a diameter of 7 cm (3 inches) and a
depth of 6 cm (2½ inches).

Peel and core the apples. Slice them thickly into a saucepan and add the lemon
juice and granulated sugar. Poach for a few minutes until the slices are just
tender but still retain their shape. Using a slotted spoon, remove the slices from
the pan and divide them evenly between the ramekins.

Whip the cream in a bowl until thick. Smooth it over the top of the apples in
each dish. Sprinkle the demerara sugar thickly over the top of the cream to
cover it completely, then put the dishes under the hot grill until the topping
caramelizes – it will appear to melt. Allow the puddings to cool a little, if you
want to serve them hot, but I think Apple Brûlée is better served cold. The
caramel topping sets hard, and will need to be struck firmly with a spoon (as
when cracking an egg) so that it breaks to reveal the smooth, creamy apple
mixture beneath.

Serves 4

500 G (1 LB) EATING APPLES

1 TABLESPOON LEMON JUICE

50 G (2 OZ) GRANULATED

SUGAR

300 ML (½ PINT) DOUBLE

CREAM

ABOUT 250 G (8 OZ)

DEMERARA SUGAR

Left: *Apple Brûlée*

Express Apple Tart

This is a good quick standby that never fails. Make it with 2 large or 3 small pears if preferred; it will not be necessary to peel them, as the skins soften during baking. The tart will feed 4 hungry people and is best eaten fresh from the oven.

1 TABLESPOON SOFT DARK
BROWN SUGAR

2 EATING APPLES

2 EGGS

3 TABLESPOONS
VEGETABLE OIL

4 TABLESPOONS CASTER SUGAR

2 TABLESPOONS DAIRY OR
SOYA MILK

½ TEASPOON VANILLA ESSENCE

5 TABLESPOONS SELF-RAISING
FLOUR

Line a 20 cm (8 inch) round flan dish with nonstick baking paper or foil, then sprinkle evenly with the brown sugar. Quarter, peel and thinly slice the apples. Arrange the slices neatly on the base of the dish, over the sugar.

Whisk the eggs and oil together in a bowl. Add the sugar, milk, vanilla essence and flour and mix well. Pour this mixture carefully over the apple, taking care not to spoil any design you have made.

Bake in a preheated oven, 200°C (400°F), Gas Mark 6, for 30 minutes, by which time the filling should be dark golden brown and springy to the touch. Cool in the dish for 2-3 minutes, then invert the tart on a serving plate. Serve with cream, custard or Apple Juice Sauce (see recipe below).

Serves 4

Apple Juice Sauce

This useful variation on cream or custard is suitable for anyone who cannot eat dairy products.

300 ML (½ PINT) APPLE JUICE

1 TABLESPOON HONEY

5 TEASPOONS ARROWROOT

5 TABLESPOONS WATER

Heat the apple juice and honey gently in a saucepan, stirring occasionally until the honey has dissolved. In a small bowl, mix the arrowroot and the measured water to a smooth paste, then stir the mixture into the hot juice. Bring to the boil, stirring constantly until the sauce thickens and clears. Simmer for a few seconds, then transfer to a jug and serve.

Serves 4

Apple Coconut Crisp

This recipe was given to me by the actress Dora Bryan, who was given it by her mother – so it has certainly stood the test of time!

Lightly grease a large ovenproof dish. Peel and core the apples. Slice them into a saucepan. Add the granulated sugar and just enough water to wet the base of the pan and prevent the apples from sticking when the sugar melts. Cook the apples for about 5 minutes, until the slices are beginning to soften but still retain their shape.

Spoon the apple mixture over the base of the dish. In a bowl, stir the baking powder and the ground rice together until thoroughly mixed; add the coconut. Cream the margarine and sugar together in a mixing bowl, until pale and fluffy. Add the almond essence. Beat in a little of the dry mixture, then add about a quarter of the beaten eggs; mix well. Continue to add alternate amounts of dry mixture and eggs until all the ingredients have been used.

Spoon the filling over the apples in the prepared dish; smooth the top. Bake in a preheated oven, 200°C (400°F), Gas Mark 6, for 20-30 minutes or until the filling is crisp and golden brown. Serve warm, with custard or cream, if liked.

Serves 6

1 KG (2 LB) BRAMLEY APPLES
125 G (4 OZ) GRANULATED SUGAR
1 TEASPOON BAKING POWDER
50 G (2 OZ) GROUND RICE
125 G (4 OZ) DESICCATED COCONUT
125 G (4 OZ) SOFT MARGARINE
125 G (4 OZ) CASTER SUGAR
FEW DROPS OF ALMOND ESSENCE
2 EGGS, BEATEN

Apple & Lemon Soufflé

11 G (½ OZ) SACHET
POWDERED GELATINE
GRATED RIND AND JUICE OF
1 LEMON
4 EGGS, SEPARATED
300 ML (½ PINT) SWEETENED
APPLE PURÉE
300 ML (½ PINT) DOUBLE
CREAM

To make this successfully, you need a measured amount of apple purée. The amount yielded by individual apples will vary according to the juiciness of the fruit but, as a rough guide, you will need about 625 g (1¼ lb). Quarter and core the apples, then chop them roughly, without peeling, into a saucepan. Add a little water and simmer for 10 minutes, by which time the fruit should be soft enough to press through a sieve into a measuring jug. Sweeten the hot purée by stirring in caster sugar or honey to taste.

Prepare a 15 cm (6 inch) round soufflé dish by tying a double thickness of greaseproof paper or baking paper around it; the paper collar should extend about 5 cm (2 inches) above the rim of the dish.

Sprinkle the gelatine on to the lemon juice in a small heatproof bowl. Set aside until spongy, then place the bowl over simmering water, stirring until the gelatine has completely dissolved.

Combine the egg yolks, apple purée and lemon rind in a larger heatproof bowl. Place over a saucepan of simmering water and whisk the mixture until it starts to thicken. Remove from the heat and continue to whisk the mixture as it cools.

Whip the cream in a large bowl until soft peaks form. In a separate, grease-free bowl, whisk the egg whites until stiff. Stir the gelatine into the apple mixture, then fold in the cream followed by the beaten egg whites.

Pour the mixture into the prepared soufflé dish. Refrigerate until set. Just before serving, carefully remove the paper collar. Decorate the soufflé with whipped cream, if liked.

Serves 4

Right: *Apple & Lemon Soufflé*

Apple Snow

4 SHARP, CRISP EATING
APPLES, SUCH AS GRANNY
SMITH
4 TABLESPOONS WATER
4 EGG WHITES
125 G (4 OZ) CASTER SUGAR

It is always useful to have some ideas for using up the egg whites left over after yolks have been used to enrich sauces and custards. Make this dessert shortly before serving, as it does not stand well for long.

Peel and core the apples. Slice them into a saucepan and add the measured water. Cook until soft, then purée in a blender or food processor.

Whisk the egg whites in a grease-free bowl until stiff, then gradually add the sugar, whisking until the mixture becomes stiff and glossy. Fold in the apple purée, pile into glass dessert dishes, and serve.

Serves 4

Cider Baked Apples

4 CRISP EATING APPLES
4 TABLESPOONS DRIED FRUIT
4 TABLESPOONS HONEY
4 TABLESPOONS CIDER

Core the apples. With a sharp knife, score the skin in a circle just above the 'equator' on each apple. Stand the apples in an ovenproof dish and then fill the centres with the dried fruit. Drizzle the honey over the apples, and pour the cider around them.

Bake in a preheated oven, 200°C (400°F), Gas Mark 6, for 30-40 minutes, until tender right through. Baste at least once during cooking, spooning the juice into the centres. Serve hot or cold.

Serves 4

Devonshire In & Out

The traditional home of this pudding is Exmoor, where every farm seems to have its own version. The name probably comes from the way the slices of apple are half in and half out of the sponge.

Peel and core the apples. Slice them thickly in crescents into a large, shallow ovenproof dish. In a bowl, mix the cinnamon with 50 g (2 oz) of the demerara sugar and then sprinkle the mixture evenly over the apple slices.

In a large mixing bowl, cream the butter with the remaining sugar. Add the beaten eggs, a little at a time, beating well after each addition and adding a little flour to the creamed mixture alternately with the eggs until all the eggs and flour have been used. Stir in the ground almonds. This should give you a fairly thick mixture, which you can drop in spoonfuls over the sliced apples; do not worry if they are not totally covered, as this creates the in-and-out effect. Sprinkle the flaked almonds evenly over the top of the dish.

Bake the pudding in a preheated oven, 180°C (350°F), Gas Mark 4, for 50-60 minutes. Serve warm, preferably with clotted cream.

Serves 6

750 G (1½ LB) COOKING APPLES
I TEASPOON GROUND CINNAMON
175 G (6 OZ) DEMERARA SUGAR
125 G (4 OZ) BUTTER, SOFTENED
2 EGGS, BEATEN
125 G (4 OZ) SELF-RAISING FLOUR
50 G (2 OZ) GROUND ALMONDS
25 G (I OZ) FLAKED ALMONDS

Peasant Girl In a Veil

1 KG (2 LB) COOKING APPLES

2 TABLESPOONS GRANULATED

SUGAR

125 G (4 OZ) PUMPERNICKEL

OR BROWN BREAD

50 G (2 OZ) DEMERARA SUGAR

150 ML (¼ PINT) THICK

YOGURT

1 CHOCOLATE FLAKE,

TO DECORATE

I think this dish originated in Eastern Europe, because of the crumbed pumpernickel, which is better than brown bread if you can get it, having a stickier texture and nutty taste. The veil is the white topping over the humble base, and my children loved it when they were young. Sophie called it pleasant girl by mistake, and the name has stuck for us.

Peel and core the apples. Slice them into a saucepan and add the sugar, with just enough water to cover the base of the pan. Cook over a moderate heat for about 10 minutes, until the apples form a pulp. Remove the pan from the heat and allow the apples to cool slightly.

Crumb the pumpernickel or brown bread in a food processor. Spread out the crumbs in a grill pan, sprinkle the demerara sugar over the top and mix lightly. Place under a moderately hot grill, frequently turning the mixture with a wooden spoon, until the sugar melts into the crumbs.

You are now ready to assemble the dish, which I serve in a lipped glass cake stand; any fairly shallow dish will do, but a glass one will show off the layers. Spread the apple in a layer over the base, and sprinkle the toasted crumbs on top. Spoon the yogurt into the centre and spread it out carefully towards the sides – this method prevents the yogurt from sticking to the crumbs. Sprinkle the top with the crumbled chocolate Flake.

Chill the pudding in the refrigerator for at least 1 hour before serving. This needs no accompaniment, and is a delicious combination of flavours.

Serves 4-6

Bramble & Apple Betty

*Whether you call them blackberries or brambles, it is a great pleasure
to take a walk in late summer or early autumn and gather these
delicious fruit for free.*

Peel and core the apples. Slice them into a large saucepan. Add the prepared
blackberries, sugar and the measured water. Simmer for 5-10 minutes, or until
the fruit is just tender. Leave to cool.

Meanwhile, melt the butter in a separate saucepan, add the breadcrumbs and
brown sugar and mix lightly.

Assemble the dessert, either in 1 large glass bowl, or in 4 individual ones. Layer
the fruit and crumb mixtures alternately, ending with a layer of crumbs. Chill
in the refrigerator for several hours or overnight. Serve chilled.

Decorate the dessert with whirls of whipped cream topped with blackberries
dusted lightly in icing sugar.

Serves 4

500 G (1 LB) COOKING APPLES

250 G (8 OZ) PREPARED

BLACKBERRIES

50 G (2 OZ) GRANULATED

SUGAR

2 TABLESPOONS WATER

50 G (2 OZ) BUTTER

175 G (6 OZ) FRESH WHITE OR

WHOLEMEAL BREADCRUMBS

50 G (2 OZ) SOFT BROWN

SUGAR

TO DECORATE

WHIPPED CREAM

BLACKBERRIES

ICING SUGAR

The Best Apple Pie

500 G (1 LB) BRAMLEY APPLES

ABOUT 2 TABLESPOONS SUGAR

150 G (5 OZ) SELF-RAISING

FLOUR

PINCH OF SALT

50 G (2 OZ) LARD, CUBED

15 G (½ OZ) HARD

MARGARINE, CUBED

1 TABLESPOON MILK, FOR

BRUSHING

It is fairly generally acknowledged in our house that the best apple pies in the North of England are made by my mother-in-law. So here is her recipe, and I only hope that your pastry turns out as mouthwateringly short as hers.

Peel and core the apples. Slice them into a saucepan in which you have put about 1 tablespoon of water. Add the sugar and cook for 5-10 minutes, until the apples start to collapse. Set aside to cool while making the pastry.

Put the flour and salt in a bowl. Add the cubes of lard and margarine and, using your fingertips, rub the fat into the flour until no large lumps remain and the mixture resembles fine breadcrumbs. Bind this together to form a stiff dough as little cold water as possible and mixing it lightly with a fork.

Divide the pastry in 2, and roll out 1 half on a lightly floured surface to a circle a little larger than a 20 cm (8 inch) round pie plate. Lift the pastry to size on to the plate and trim to fit, then put the cooled apples over this, leaving the pastry edge clear.

Roll out the remaining pastry to make a lid, fit it over the apples and trim to size. Seal the edges by pressing the 2 layers of pastry together with your thumb and index finger.

Brush the top of the pie with a little milk. Bake in a preheated oven, 200°C (400°F), Gas Mark 6, for 30 minutes or until the crust is golden. The pie may be eaten hot or cold, and is often accompanied in the North by a piece of cheese.

Serves 4-6

Spiced Apple Slices

You can serve this on its own, or with the conventional cream, yogurt or custard sauce, but for a real taste sensation, try it with Honey Saffron Custard (see page 65).

Peel and core the apples. Slice them thickly into a large bowl and then toss with a little of the lemon juice to prevent them from discolouring. Use the butter to grease a shallow baking dish, then arrange a layer of apple slices on the base. Sprinkle with about half the lemon rind and juice, then add half the demerara sugar and ground cinnamon. Top with the remaining apple slices. Sprinkle with the remaining lemon rind, lemon juice, sugar and cinnamon.

Cover the dish with a lid or foil and bake the dessert in a preheated oven, 190°C (375°F), Gas Mark 5, for 30 minutes, turning the apple slices in the juice several times during the cooking time to ensure that they are evenly coated in the liquid. Serve the dessert warm or cold with cream, ice cream, crème fraîche or Honey Saffron Custard, if liked.

Serves 4

750 G (1½ LB) COOKING
APPLES
GRATED RIND AND JUICE
OF 1 LEMON
25 G (1 OZ) BUTTER
175 G (6 OZ) DEMERARA
SUGAR
1 TEASPOON GROUND
CINNAMON

Swiss Apple Flan

RICH SHORTCRUST PASTRY

175 G (6 OZ) PLAIN FLOUR

25 G (1 OZ) ICING SUGAR

25 G (1 OZ) GROUND ALMONDS

125 G (4 OZ) BUTTER, DICED

1 EGG YOLK

1 TABLESPOON COLD WATER

FILLING

1 KG (2 LB) COOKING APPLES

2 TABLESPOONS LEMON JUICE

4 TABLESPOONS GRANULATED

SUGAR

25 G (1 OZ) FRESH WHITE

BREADCRUMBS

50 G (2 OZ) CHOPPED

ALMONDS, TOASTED

125 G (4 OZ) FLAKED

ALMONDS

50 G (2 OZ) CASTER SUGAR

Some apple pies have so many additional ingredients that you can't taste the apples. This is not the case with this recipe, however, where the other flavours accentuate the apple flavour.

Make the pastry. Sift the flour and icing sugar into a bowl, then stir in the ground almonds. Rub in the butter with your fingertips until the mixture resembles fine breadcrumbs. Add the egg yolk and cold water and mix to a soft dough. This pastry is easy to make in a food processor: process the flour, sugar, ground almonds and butter until crumbed, then add the egg yolk and water through the feeder tube with the motor running. Knead the pastry briefly on a lightly floured surface until it forms a smooth ball, then wrap it in clingfilm and refrigerate for at least 30 minutes.

Meanwhile, prepare the filling. Peel and core the apples and slice into a pan; add the lemon juice and granulated sugar. Place over a gentle heat until the slices are beginning to soften but still retain their shape. With a slotted spoon, transfer the apple slices to a plate and leave to cool.

Roll out the pastry on a lightly floured surface and use to line a 23 cm (9 inch) round flan tin. Mix the breadcrumbs with the chopped toasted almonds and spread this mixture over the pastry base. Arrange the apple slices evenly on top. Mix the flaked almonds and caster sugar in a bowl. Stir in a spoonful of water to dissolve the sugar, then drizzle this topping over the apple slices.

Bake in a preheated oven, 190°C (375°F), Gas Mark 5, for 40 minutes, covering the dish with foil if the flaked almonds start to scorch. Serve hot.

Serves 6-8

Right: *Swiss Apple Flan*

Apple Strudel

175 G (6 OZ) FILO PASTRY,
THAWED IF FROZEN

75 G (3 OZ) BUTTER, MELTED

50 G (2 OZ) FRESH WHITE
BREADCRUMBS

750 G (1½ LB) COOKING
APPLES, PEELED, CORED AND
SLICED

50 G (2 OZ) SULTANAS

75 G (3 OZ) CASTER SUGAR

50 G (2 OZ) WALNUTS,
CHOPPED

1 TEASPOON MIXED SPICE

ICING SUGAR, FOR DUSTING

How many versions of apple strudel have you tasted? I'd be quite happy to go on trying different ones for the rest of my life, but perhaps it is time to call a halt and suggest that we take advantage of the excellent ready-made filo pastry now available to make this the definitive version.

Grease a large baking sheet. Spread half the filo pastry on to a clean tea towel, overlapping the sheets slightly to make a rectangle measuring about 50 x 45 cm (20 x 18 inches). Brush lightly with melted butter. Place the rest of the filo on top, brushing the surface with melted butter, then scatter the breadcrumbs over the top. Arrange the apples evenly over the pastry, leaving a 5 cm (2 inch) border all round.

Mix the sultanas, caster sugar, chopped walnuts and mixed spice in a bowl. Sprinkle the mixture over the apple slices.

Roll up the pastry firmly over the filling, as when making a Swiss roll, using the tea towel as a guide. Transfer the strudel to the prepared baking sheet, curving the roll slightly to make a horseshoe shape. Brush the top of the pastry with the remaining melted butter.

Bake in a preheated oven, 190°C (375°F), Gas Mark 5, for 35-40 minutes or until crisp and golden brown. Serve warm, dusted with icing sugar.

Serves 8

Eve's Pudding

This is a classic temptation – tasty apples baked with a touch of cloves, and a soft sponge topping with a crisp crust. Do use tasty apples, such as Cox's, rather than the baking ones. They will need little, if any, additional sugar.

Grease a 1.2 litre (2 pint) ovenproof dish. In a large mixing bowl, cream the butter and caster sugar together until pale and fluffy. Add the lemon rind. Stir in the eggs, a little at a time, then fold in the flour and salt.

Peel and core the apples. Slice them on to the base of the dish. Mix the cloves with the granulated sugar in a small bowl. Stir in the lemon juice. Drizzle the mixture over the apple slices, then stir lightly to mix.

Spoon the sponge mixture over the sliced apples. Smooth the surface, but don't worry if it is not level – it will even out during cooking.

Bake in a preheated oven, 180°C (350°F), Gas Mark 4, for about 40 minutes or until the top of the sponge is golden brown and springy to the touch. Serve hot or warm, with cream.

Serves 4-6

Variation

This is delicious when made with the first shoots of tender, forced rhubarb. You may need to increase the sugar for the base to 175 g (6 oz), and I think a teaspoon of ground ginger goes better with the flavour of rhubarb than the ground cloves.

125 G (4 OZ) BUTTER, SOFTENED
125 G (4 OZ) CASTER SUGAR
GRATED RIND AND JUICE OF 1 LEMON
2 EGGS, BEATEN
250 G (8 OZ) SELF-RAISING FLOUR
PINCH OF SALT
750 G (1½ LB) EATING APPLES
½ TEASPOON GROUND CLOVES
50 G (2 OZ) GRANULATED SUGAR

Apple Hat

175 G (6 OZ) SELF-RAISING
FLOUR

PINCH OF SALT

50 G (2 OZ) FRESH WHITE
BREADCRUMBS

125 G (4 OZ) SHREDDED SUET

ABOUT 150 ML (¼ PINT) MILK

750 G (1½ LB) COOKING
APPLES

4 TABLESPOONS DEMERARA
SUGAR

75 ML (3 FL OZ) WATER,

150 ML (¼ PINT) SINGLE
CREAM, TO SERVE

When I was a child and my mother brought this pudding to the table, my father would always insist we held our ears out on either side of our heads and shout 'apple hat'. Where did this strange ritual originate? I repeat it in the hope that someone will tell me their family did the same thing, and I will feel part of some great, if obscure, folk tradition, rather than just the child of a charming eccentric.

Grease a 1 litre (1¾ pint) pudding basin. Mix the flour, salt, breadcrumbs and suet in a bowl. Mix in just enough of the milk to form a soft dough. On a lightly floured surface, roll or pat out two-thirds of the dough and line the prepared pudding basin. Set the remaining dough aside.

Peel and core the apples. Slice into the dough-lined basin. Add 3 tablespoons of the demerara sugar and the measured water. Roll out the rest of the pastry to make a lid, and press this over the top of the apple filling, squeezing the edges together between your thumb and index finger to give a good seal.

Cover the top of the basin with a piece of greased foil, pleated in the centre to allow the pudding to rise; twist the edges of the foil under the rim of the basin to make a secure lid. Stand the pudding basin on a trivet or upturned saucer in a large saucepan, and pour in boiling water to about 4 cm (1½ inches) from the top of the basin. Return to the boil, then lower the heat and simmer for 3 hours, topping up the water as required. Alternatively, cook the pudding in the microwave for 10 minutes on High, then stand for 5 minutes; this will not give quite as light a texture.

Allow the pudding to stand for a few minutes before loosening the edges with a knife and turning it out on a serving plate. Sprinkle the remaining demerara sugar over the top, and pour cream around the base. Ear waggling is optional.

Serves 8

Nutty Apple Crumble

*No chapter of apple recipes would be complete without an apple crumble –
this one has a delicious crunchy topping that includes oats and nuts.*

Peel and core the apples and slice them into a large ovenproof dish. Spread them out to cover the base of the dish, then sprinkle the granulated sugar evenly over the apple slices.

Put the flour, oats, demerara sugar, nuts and butter or margarine in a food processor and process briefly to create a rubbed-in mixture without losing all the texture of the oats and nuts. Alternatively, this may be done by hand, by placing all the dry ingredients in a large mixing bowl then rubbing in the butter or margarine; in this case the oats will remain whole, giving the topping a coarser texture.

Sprinkle the topping evenly over the apple slices and bake the crumble in a preheated oven, 200°C (400°F), Gas Mark 6, for about 30-40 minutes, until the topping is golden brown and the apples are tender. Serve the crumble warm with cream or ice cream, if liked.

Serves 6

750 G (1½ LB) COOKING APPLES

50 G (2 OZ) GRANULATED SUGAR

75 G (3 OZ) WHOLEMEAL FLOUR

50 G (2 OZ) ROLLED OATS

75 G (3 OZ) DEMERARA SUGAR

50 G (2 OZ) CHOPPED MIXED NUTS

75 G (3 OZ) BUTTER OR MARGARINE

Apple Charlotte

750 G (1½ LB) COOKING
APPLES
1 TABLESPOON LEMON JUICE
125 G (4 OZ) GRANULATED
SUGAR
125 G (4 OZ) BUTTER,
SOFTENED
12 SLICES OF WHITE OR
WHOLEMEAL BREAD, CRUSTS
REMOVED
50 G (2 OZ) DEMERARA SUGAR

You can't beat this for sheer old-fashioned comfort food – everyone likes it.

Peel and core the apples and then slice them into a large saucepan with the lemon juice and granulated sugar. Cook over a gentle heat until the apples start to collapse. Beat the apple mixture thoroughly to form a purée.

Butter the bread generously. Arrange 4 slices, butter side down, over the base of a large, shallow ovenproof dish. Spread half of the apple purée over the bread, then add another layer of 4 slices of bread, this time butter side up. Spread the rest of the apple purée over the bread layer, and then finish with the last 4 slices of bread, butter side up. Sprinkle the demerara sugar evenly over the top of the dish.

Bake the charlotte in a preheated oven, 190°C (375°F), Gas Mark 5, for about 40 minutes, or until the top is crisp and golden brown. Serve hot with custard, cream or ice cream.

Serves 4-6

Tokamak

The name relates to a sort of doughnut-shaped reactor which my daughter's boyfriend is working on to help create nuclear fusion and thus save the world – I think. Anyway, the shape is echoed in this fruity dessert.

Cut the apples in half around the 'equator', and take out the cores. Mix the lemon juice, brown sugar and measured water together in an ovenproof dish large enough to hold all the apple halves in a single layer. Arrange the apple halves on the base of the dish, cut side down. Bake in a preheated oven, 200°C (400°F), Gas Mark 6, for 10 minutes.

Remove the dish from the oven and turn the apples cut side up. Baste with the cooking juices, then lay a pineapple ring on top of each apple half. Return the dish to the oven for 5 minutes while making the meringue.

Whisk the egg whites in a grease-free bowl until stiff, then gradually whisk in the sugar until firm and glossy. Fold in the nuts. Remove the dish from the oven and pile the meringue mixture on to each pineapple-topped apple. Some of the meringue will ooze down the centre of the pineapple rings; when this cooks it will give each pudding a mushroom shape.

Return to the oven and bake for 10 minutes more, until the meringue is crisply browned and the apples are tender. Serve on individual plates, with a little of the cooking juices spooned around. This is delicious with a little thick cream.

Serves 4

2 LARGE COOKING APPLES

1 TABLESPOON LEMON JUICE

1 TABLESPOON SOFT DARK BROWN SUGAR

2 TABLESPOONS WATER

4 FRESH OR DRAINED CANNED PINEAPPLE RINGS

2 EGG WHITES

125 G (4 OZ) CASTER SUGAR

25 G (1 OZ) HAZELNUTS, TOASTED AND CHOPPED

Around the World

Zabaglione

This rich dessert originated in Milan, northern Italy, and provides the perfect conclusion to an Italian meal. Always make it just before serving and serve in barely warm glasses or dishes. It can also be served as a topping for ice cream or fruit. Be careful not to cook this dessert too long or it will separate out. There are many variations to Zabaglione such as flavouring it with a teaspoon of vanilla essence or adding strawberry pieces to the bottom of the glass and spooning the Zabaglione mixture on top. Marsala is the classic base for this dessert but different wines or spirits can be used instead, such as champagne, sherry or rum.

Put the egg yolks in a large heatproof bowl with the sugar and beat until the sugar has dissolved and the mixture is pale and frothy. Add a little of the marsala, whisk again, then stand the bowl over a pan of barely simmering water. Continue to whisk, gradually adding the remaining marsala, until the mixture is thick and foamy; this will take about 5 minutes. Use a hand-held electric mixer if you have one.

Serve at once, in stemmed glasses, with biscuits or sponge fingers for dipping.

Serves 4

4 EGG YOLKS

125 G (4 OZ) CASTER SUGAR

175 ML (6 FL OZ) MARSALA

THIN CRISP ALMOND BISCUITS

OR SPONGE FINGERS,

TO SERVE

Left: *Zabaglione*

Pashka

50 G (2 OZ) MIXED
CANDIED PEEL
50 G (2 OZ) CRYSTALLIZED
GINGER
50 G (2 OZ) GLACÉ PINEAPPLE
50 G (2 OZ) ALMONDS,
TOASTED AND CHOPPED
625 G (1¼ LB) COTTAGE
CHEESE
150 ML (¼ PINT) SOURED
CREAM OR DOUBLE CREAM
WITH A DASH OF LEMON
JUICE
50 G (2 OZ) BUTTER,
SOFTENED
75 G (3 OZ) CASTER SUGAR
I TEASPOON VANILLA ESSENCE
GLACÉ CHERRIES, WHOLE
ALMONDS AND GLACÉ FRUITS,
TO DECORATE

This Russian speciality is traditionally eaten at Easter. Special moulds in the shape of pyramids are conventionally used, but you may find it easier to make the pudding in a circular colander or sieve, which is what I do, or attempt Russian authenticity with a conical sieve – whatever you use as a mould must have holes to allow the whey to drain.

If you have a piece of cheesecloth big enough to line your colander or large sieve, use this, otherwise a clean tea towel will suffice. Pour boiling water over the cloth to scald it, then wring it out and line the colander or sieve.

Cut the candied peel, crystallized ginger and glacé pineapple into small chunks of about the same size. Set aside in a large bowl, with the almonds.

Put the cottage cheese, soured cream, butter, sugar and vanilla essence into a food processor and process until smooth. Alternatively, cream the butter with the sugar in a large bowl, sieve in the cottage cheese, then beat in the rest of the ingredients. Stir the mixture into the bowl containing the mixed fruits.

Spoon into the lined colander or sieve, smooth the top and fold the edges of the cloth over. Press a plate of suitable size on top of the pudding and add a light weight – about 250 g (8 oz) should be enough. Set the colander or sieve over a bowl to catch the whey, and leave in a cool larder or refrigerator overnight.

To serve, remove the weighted plate, unfold the cloth and turn the pashka out on to a serving dish or platter. Decorate with a selection of fruits and nuts in a fairly formal pattern – a crown or jewelled Fabergé egg is the traditional design – or you can make flower shapes using cherries as centres and whole almonds for the petals. Serve the pashka in slices.

Serves 6

Irish Coffee Cheesecake

This has a rich, smooth taste and makes an appropriate finish to a meal for St Patrick's day.

Make the base. Crumb the biscuits in a food processor, or place in a strong polythene bag and crush with a rolling pin. Melt the butter in a saucepan over a gentle heat, then stir in the crumbs until well coated. Press the mixture over the base of a greased 25 cm (10 inch) round loose-bottomed cake tin and then chill in the refrigerator.

Make the filling. Combine the marshmallows, milk, caster sugar and coffee granules in a saucepan. Stir over a gentle heat until the marshmallows have melted. Pour the mixture into a bowl and leave to cool.

Beat the cream cheese and whiskey in a bowl until smooth, and mix this into the cooled marshmallow mixture. Chill until on the point of setting. Whip the cream until it stands in soft peaks, then fold thoroughly into the almost-set mixture. Pour over the base and return to the refrigerator until set.

Remove the cheesecake from the tin, transfer it to a serving plate and smooth the sides with a knife. Decorate with whirls of whipped cream, each topped with a coffee bean, and add some miniature marshmallows. Serve chilled.

Serves 6

BASE

175 G (6 OZ) DIGESTIVE BISCUITS

75 G (3 OZ) BUTTER

FILLING

250 G (8 OZ) WHITE MARSHMALLOWS

75 ML (3 FL OZ) MILK

50 G (2 OZ) CASTER SUGAR

2½ TEASPOONS INSTANT COFFEE GRANULES

50 G (2 OZ) CREAM CHEESE

3 TABLESPOONS IRISH WHISKEY

300 ML (½ PINT) DOUBLE CREAM

TO DECORATE

WHIPPED CREAM

COFFEE BEANS

MINIATURE PINK AND WHITE MARSHMALLOWS

Tarte au Citron

RICH SWEET PASTRY

175 G (6 OZ) PLAIN FLOUR

I TEASPOON CASTER SUGAR

75 G (3 OZ) BUTTER

I EGG YOLK

FILLING

2 EGGS

50 G (2 OZ) CASTER SUGAR

50 G (2 OZ) GROUND ALMONDS

FINELY GRATED RIND AND

JUICE OF 2 LEMONS

ICING SUGAR, FOR DUSTING

Although this recipe is a classic from the South of France, I first tasted it in Manchester, at the home of my friend Shelley Rohde. Shelley also has a house in Provence, which is where she obtained the recipe. She recommends using organically grown lemons if you can get them, or at least lemons which have not been waxed, as the rind will have a better flavour. Failing this, wash the lemons well before grating them as finely as possible.

Make the pastry. Mix the flour and the sugar together in a bowl and rub in the butter until the mixture resembles fine breadcrumbs. Using a fork, bind the mixture with the egg yolk, adding a little cold water only if necessary to make the pastry form a ball. Alternatively, use a food processor: process the flour, sugar and butter together, then add the egg yolk through the feeder tube, with the motor running. Add a little water only if necessary.

Wrap the pastry and chill it in the refrigerator for 20 minutes, then roll out on a lightly floured surface and use to line a 20 cm (8 inch) round pie dish. Line the base with foil, add baking beans and bake blind in a preheated oven, 200°F (400°F), Gas Mark 6, for 10 minutes. Remove the baking beans and foil and then return the pastry case to the oven for 5 minutes to crisp the base. Leave to cool a little while making the filling.

Whisk the eggs and caster sugar together in a bowl until pale and foamy; the whisk should leave a trail when lifted and the mixture should almost double in bulk. Add the ground almonds, lemon rind and juice; mix well.

Pour the filling into the pastry case. Bake at 180°C (350°F), Gas Mark 4, for about 30 minutes, or until the filling is just set. Cool slightly, then dust with icing sugar and serve at once.

Serves 6

Zuppa Inglese

I simply don't understand the name of this dessert. It means English soup and yet is neither of these things. When I asked an Italian friend for an explanation, he replied gloomily that it was a sort of trifle, and very boring. I assure you that he changed his mind after trying this version.

Arrange the slices of Swiss roll around the base and sides of a large glass bowl. Sprinkle with two-thirds of the Amaretto.

Melt the chocolate with the coffee in a heatproof bowl over a saucepan of barely simmering water. Add the remaining Amaretto and mix to a smooth sauce. Leave to cool slightly, then beat in the egg yolks.

Whip the cream in a bowl until soft peaks form, then fold it into the chocolate mixture. Whisk the egg whites in a separate, grease-free bowl; fold them into the mixture. Pour the filling over the soaked Swiss roll slices and chill in the refrigerator for several hours.

Before serving, top the Zuppa Inglese with whirls of whipped cream topped with crystallized violets. Add some small ratafias.

Serves 8

1 SMALL CHOCOLATE SWISS ROLL, SLICED

75 ML (3 FL OZ) AMARETTO

125 G (4 OZ) PLAIN CHOCOLATE, BROKEN INTO SQUARES

1 TABLESPOON STRONG BLACK COFFEE

150 ML (¼ PINT) DOUBLE CREAM

3 EGGS, SEPARATED

TO DECORATE

WHIPPED CREAM

CRYSTALLIZED VIOLETS

SMALL RATAFIA BISCUITS

Tiramisu

4 TRIFLE SPONGES

2 TABLESPOONS STRONG
BLACK COFFEE

2 TABLESPOONS AMARETTO

200 G (7 OZ) MASCARPONE

2 TABLESPOONS CASTER SUGAR

COCOA POWDER, FOR DUSTING

CHOCOLATE SAUCE

125 G (4 OZ) PLAIN
CHOCOLATE, BROKEN INTO
SQUARES

1 TABLESPOON SINGLE CREAM

1 TABLESPOON AMARETTO

I can still remember the first time I tasted this, at the end of a long hot day in Tuscany. The name translates as pick-me-up and I can testify that it certainly does just that.

Slice the trifle sponges in half horizontally. Mix the coffee with the Amaretto in a jug; then sprinkle over both halves of each sponge. Beat the mascarpone and caster sugar in a large bowl and use this to sandwich the halves of soaked sponge together in pairs. Place the 'sandwiches' on a large plate and spread the remaining mascarpone mixture over the surface of each. Using a sieve, dust lightly with cocoa powder.

Make the chocolate sauce.Put the chocolate, cream and Amaretto in a large heatproof bowl and place over a saucepan of barely simmering water.Leave until cool and then stir until smooth.

Flood 4 individual serving plates with the chocolate sauce, then using a fish slice, carefully transfer a portion of tiramisu to each plate. Serve at once.

Serves 4

Portuguese Walnut Pudding

Grind the walnuts finely in a food processor. In a large bowl, whisk the eggs, caster sugar and cinnamon together. Add the ground nuts and mix well. Spoon the mixture into a 20 cm (8 inch) round soufflé dish, and stand the dish in a roasting tin. Pour in hot water to a depth of 5 cm (2 inches).

Bake in a preheated oven, 180°C (350°F), Gas Mark 4, for about 1½ hours or until a knife inserted in the centre of the pudding comes out clean. Leave to cool, then refrigerate for 2-3 hours. Decorate with whipped cream and walnut halves, or with a selection of fresh fruit slices.

Serves 4-6

175 G (6 OZ) WALNUTS

5 EGGS

250 G (8 OZ) CASTER SUGAR

I TEASPOON GROUND

CINNAMON

TO SERVE

WHIPPED CREAM

WALNUT HALVES

Shrikand

Is this Indian or Persian in origin? Perhaps it is one of the many dishes that the Moghul emperors brought to northern India. It certainly has all the taste and aroma of the mysterious East.

Infuse the saffron in the boiling water in a heatproof bowl for 10 minutes. Add the rosewater.

Split the cardamom pods with the point of a sharp knife and remove the dark brown or black seeds. Crush these, preferably with a pestle in a mortar, and add to the saffron mixture.

Tip the yogurt into a bowl, sprinkle over the icing sugar, add the spice mixture and fold together. Spoon into 4 glasses and chill. Before serving, sprinkle the toasted chopped pistachio nuts over each portion.

Serves 4

½ TEASPOON POWDERED

SAFFRON

I TABLESPOON BOILING

WATER

2½ TEASPOONS

CONCENTRATED ROSEWATER

3 GREEN CARDAMOM PODS

600 ML (I PINT) THICK

YOGURT, CHILLED

I TABLESPOON ICING SUGAR

2 TABLESPOONS PISTACHIO

NUTS, TOASTED AND CHOPPED

Overleaf, Left: *Bavarois*

Right: *Tarte au Citron*

Normandy Apples
with Cream Cheese

1 KG (2 LB) APPLES

25 G (1 OZ) BUTTER

250 ML (8 FL OZ) APPLE
JUICE

½ TEASPOON VANILLA ESSENCE

50 G (2 OZ) GRANULATED
SUGAR

150 ML (¼ PINT) DOUBLE
CREAM

125 G (4 OZ) CREAM CHEESE

2 EGGS

50 G (2 OZ) CASTER SUGAR

ICING SUGAR, FOR DREDGING

The French eat their Golden Delicious apples yellower and riper than we do, which may help to explain why these fruit get such a bad press in this country: we just don't let them mature enough. I'd suggest you use eating apples for this recipe, but they don't have to be French; our own English apples are a glorious heritage.

Peel and core the apples and coarsely chop them into a bowl. Use the butter to grease a large ovenproof dish generously, then arrange the pieces of apple over the base. Warm the apple juice in a saucepan with the vanilla essence and granulated sugar. When the sugar has melted, pour the mixture over the apples in the dish. Cover with a lid or foil and bake in a preheated oven, 190°C (375°F), Gas Mark 5, for 15 minutes.

Meanwhile, beat the cream, cream cheese, eggs and caster sugar together in a bowl. Pour this mixture over the cooked apples. Return the dish to the oven and bake, uncovered, for 20 minutes more. Serve hot, dredged with a little icing sugar.

Serves 6

Bavarois

According to legend, this classic dish was invented by a French chef who worked for a Bavarian aristocrat, and became so fond of his adopted country that he named his greatest creation after it. There are many variations on the basic theme, as the smooth light cream can be flavoured with a variety of liqueurs, or served with fruit sauces. Ring the changes yourself, mixing and matching the flavours.

½ X 11 G (½ OZ) SACHET
POWDERED GELATINE
2 TABLESPOONS WATER
2 EGG YOLKS
2 TABLESPOONS CLEAR HONEY
150 ML (¼ PINT) DOUBLE
CREAM
1 TABLESPOON BRANDY
2 TABLESPOONS GROUND
ALMONDS
FRUIT COULIS
2 PEACHES, SKINNED AND
STONED
1 TABLESPOON ICING SUGAR
2 TABLESPOONS WATER

Line the base of 4 individual ramekins with a circle of nonstick baking paper. Place the ramekins on a baking sheet. Sprinkle the gelatine on to the surface of the measured water in a cup or heatproof bowl. Set aside until spongy, then set over a small saucepan of simmering water until the gelatine has dissolved.

Combine the egg yolks and honey in a heatproof bowl over a saucepan of barely simmering water. Whisk for about 5 minutes until the mixture is pale, frothy and thick, and the whisk leaves a trail on the surface when lifted. Take the pan off the heat and gradually whisk in the dissolved gelatine. Pour the mixture into a clean bowl, which will speed the cooling process, and set aside. The mixture will start to set as it cools.

Whip the cream and brandy in a bowl until thick. Fold in the ground almonds, then fold the flavoured cream gently into the cooled egg mixture. Pour into the prepared ramekins and refrigerate for several hours until set.

Meanwhile, make the fruit coulis by puréeing all the ingredients in a blender or food processor. To unmould, run the point of a sharp knife around the edge of each bavarois, invert a plate over the top, then turn both plate and ramekin upside down and give a firm shake; the bavarois should slip out easily. Serve each portion with a little of the fruit coulis poured around.

Serves 4

Baklava

250 G (8 OZ) BUTTER

250 G (8 OZ) FILO PASTRY,
THAWED IF FROZEN

FILLING

125 G (4 OZ) PISTACHIO NUTS
OR BLANCHED ALMONDS,
FINELY CHOPPED

I TABLESPOON CASTER SUGAR

SYRUP

375 G (12 OZ) CASTER SUGAR

250 ML (8 FL OZ) WATER

I TABLESPOON LEMON JUICE

Turkish cuisine has many fascinating dishes, a tasty blend of East and West. This is a classic, perhaps the national dessert, and not too difficult to try at home now that good quality filo pastry is widely available.

Melt the butter in a small pan; brush a little of it over the base and sides of a 30 x 20 cm (12 x 8 inch) roasting tin. Using a sharp knife, cut through all the sheets of filo pastry at the same time, to a size which will generously fit the roasting tin. If you have to join some pieces, this does not matter. Cover the filo pastry with a damp tea towel to prevent it from drying out while making the filling. Mix the nuts with the sugar in a bowl. Layer half the filo pastry in the roasting tin, brushing each layer lightly with butter before adding the next. Sprinkle the filling evenly over the top, then add the remaining filo in the same way.

Clarify the remaining butter by heating it gently again in a small saucepan, skimming off any scum from the top and leaving the sediment to settle. Pour the clear liquid on top – the clarified butter – into another container.

Cut the layered and filled filo pastry in the roasting tin into small squares or diamonds, wiping the blade of the knife after each cut, and slicing through all the layers. Pour the clarified butter over the top so that it soaks into the cuts. Leave to stand for 30 minutes.

Bake the baklava in a preheated oven, 200°C (400°F), Gas Mark 6, for 30-40 minutes or until the top is crisp and golden brown.

Meanwhile, prepare the syrup. Heat the sugar, measured water and lemon juice in a saucepan and stir until the sugar has dissolved. When the syrup boils, lower the heat and simmer for 2 minutes without further stirring. Remove from the heat.

Cool the baked baklava in the tin for 5 minutes, then pour the syrup evenly over the top. Serve at room temperature.

Serves 12

Right: *Baklava*

Thai Coconut Custard

4 EGG YOLKS

125 G (4 OZ) SUGAR

400 ML (14 FL OZ) COCONUT

MILK

2 TABLESPOONS TOASTED

DESICCATED COCONUT

It is interesting to find a recipe for custard which does not use milk. We serve this with a few slices of banana, as the tastes go so well together, but pineapple and papaya would be equally appropriate, the sharpness in the fruit balancing the creamy flavour of the smooth sweet custard. You can buy canned coconut milk in Asian food stores.

Whisk the egg yolks together lightly in a large bowl. Add the sugar and whisk again. Add the coconut milk gradually, whisking well after each addition. Pour the mixture into a saucepan. Heat very gently, stirring all the time until the custard thickens. Be careful not to let the custard boil, or it will curdle. Pour the custard into a shallow serving dish, and sprinkle the desiccated coconut over the surface while still warm. Leave to cool, when the custard will thicken further and set.

Serves 4-6

Jamaican Bananas

PER PERSON:

1 BANANA

1 TABLESPOON RUM

1 TABLESPOON SOFT DARK

BROWN SUGAR

4 TEASPOONS ORANGE JUICE

1 TEASPOON BUTTER

This can be adapted to serve any number of guests.

Peel the bananas, slice them in half lengthways and arrange them in a single layer in an ovenproof dish. Add the rum, sugar and orange juice to the dish and dot the butter over the fruit. Bake in a preheated oven, 200°C (400°F), Gas Mark 6, for 10 minutes, basting the bananas with the juices halfway through cooking. Serve warm, with cream or yogurt, if liked.

Pineapple Malibu

Simply delicious – that's the best way to describe this dessert.

Peel and core the pineapple. Cut the flesh into bite-sized chunks and put these in a serving bowl. Add the coconut, Malibu and sugar. Mix well. Cover the bowl and chill in the refrigerator for 2-3 hours, stirring several times. Serve straight from the refrigerator.

Serves 4

I FRESH RIPE PINEAPPLE

2 TABLESPOONS TOASTED
DESICCATED COCONUT

5 TABLESPOONS MALIBU

2 TABLESPOONS CASTER SUGAR

Swedish Baked Plums

Cinnamon cream provides an interesting accompaniment to the flavoursome plums.

Arrange the plums, cut side up, in a single layer in a shallow ovenproof dish. Pour the red wine over, and dot the fruit with the jam. Add the orange rind and juice, and sprinkle the sugar evenly over the fruit.

Bake in a preheated oven, 190°C (375°F), Gas Mark 5, for 30 minutes, basting with the juices halfway through cooking.

Meanwhile, make the cinnamon cream. Whip the cream in a bowl until soft peaks form. Mix the honey and cinnamon in a cup, then fold the mixture into the cream.

When the plums are tender and the cooking juices concentrated, remove the baking dish from the oven. Serve hot or cold, with the cinnamon cream.

Serves 6

I KG (2 LB) PLUMS, HALVED
AND STONED

150 ML (¼ PINT) RED WINE

2 TABLESPOONS RASPBERRY
JAM

GRATED RIND AND JUICE
OF I ORANGE

I TABLESPOON SOFT DARK
BROWN SUGAR

CINNAMON CREAM

200 ML (7 FL OZ) DOUBLE
CREAM

2 TEASPOONS CLEAR HONEY

I TEASPOON GROUND
CINNAMON

Dulce de Chocolate

600 ML (1 PINT) MILK

175 G (6 OZ) SOFT DARK
BROWN SUGAR

1 TEASPOON GROUND
CINNAMON

1 TEASPOON GROUND
ALLSPICE

50 G (2 OZ) COCOA POWDER

50 G (2 OZ) CORNFLOUR

This spiced chocolate pudding comes from Mexico. It can be served hot, as a rich sauce over ice cream, or cold.

Whisk all the ingredients together in a large bowl, using a hand-held electric mixer, or a food processor. Pour the mixture into a pan. Heat gently, stirring all the time. As soon as the mixture boils and thickens, beat it vigorously to avoid the formation of lumps. Serve at once, over ice cream, if liked, or cover the surface closely and chill.

Serves 4

Danish Lemon

11 G (½ OZ) SACHET
POWDERED GELATINE

4 TABLESPOONS WATER

GRATED RIND AND JUICE
OF 2 LEMONS

5 EGGS, SEPARATED

125 G (4 OZ) SUGAR

When you make this light, tangy dessert you'll understand why the local name means can't-leave-me-alone pudding. It is best made a day before you wish to eat it, to give the flavours time to develop.

Sprinkle the gelatine on to the surface of the measured water in a heatproof bowl. Set aside until spongy, then set the bowl over a saucepan of simmering water until the gelatine has dissolved. Stir in the lemon rind and juice.

Whisk the egg yolks with the sugar in a bowl until thick, pale and foamy. Whisk in the gelatine mixture. In a separate, grease-free bowl, whisk the egg whites until stiff; fold them into the lemon mixture.

Pour the mixture into a serving dish and chill overnight in the refrigerator before serving.

Serves 6

Clafoutis

This cherry batter pudding originated in the Limousin area of France, but is now enjoyed wherever juicy dark red cherries are available. Once you master the art of removing the stones quickly with a little gadget made especially for the purpose (I have one attached to a garlic press), there is no danger of granny breaking her dentures on the cherry stones.

500 G (1 LB) DARK RED
CHERRIES, STALKS REMOVED,
STONED
2 EGGS
300 ML (½ PINT) MILK
2 TABLESPOONS CASTER SUGAR
PINCH OF SALT
125 G (4 OZ) PLAIN FLOUR

Lightly grease a 25 cm (10 inch) round flan dish. Spread the cherries over the base. Make a batter, either by whisking the eggs and milk together in a bowl and then beating in the dry ingredients, or by whizzing all the ingredients together in a blender or food processor. Strain if necessary to remove any lumps. Allow the batter to stand for 30 minutes if possible to allow the flour to absorb the liquid; beat again before using.

Pour the batter over the cherries in the dish. Bake in a preheated oven, 200°C (400°F), Gas Mark 6, for 35-45 minutes until it is just set in the centre.

Serves 6-8

Variation

If preferred, the clafoutis may be baked in 12 greased individual muffin tins. Put about 4 cherries in the base of each before pouring in the batter. Bake at the same oven temperature but for a shorter time: 25-30 minutes. The batter puffs up well when cooked in this way, and the puddings should be served at once, before they start to collapse.

Spanish Shape

375 G (12 OZ) CURD CHEESE

1 TABLESPOON CLEAR HONEY

75 G (3 OZ) PINE NUTS,
TOASTED

½ TEASPOON GROUND
CINNAMON

When I was a child, Spanish was not the name of things from Spain, but rather the word for sticks of liquorice which we bought for pennies and chewed until our mouths were a ghastly black colour – part of the attraction, I'm sure. There is no liquorice in this traditional pudding from Spain, which has an interesting blend of sweet and savoury flavours. People who claim not to have a sweet tooth will enjoy this with a selection of fresh fruits. The mixture also makes an excellent stuffing for apricot or nectarine halves.

Line a colander or sieve with a piece of muslin or cheesecloth. If you have no other suitable material, a clean tea towel will do very well. Put the cheese in the lined colander, fold the cloth over, and put a small plate on top. Add a weight of about 500 g (1 lb) and set the colander or sieve over a bowl or sink to catch the whey. Leave for at least 1 hour, then discard the whey or reserve it for use in another recipe (for making scones, perhaps).

Tip the pressed cheese into a bowl. Add the honey and mix well, then stir in the pine nuts and cinnamon. Press the mixture into a mould lined with clingfilm and chill until ready to serve.

When required, invert the pudding on a serving plate, using the clingfilm to ease it out of the mould. Decorate as desired.

Serves 6

Toffee Bananas

You wouldn't normally think of going to a Chinese restaurant specifically for the pudding. However, my husband has always considered Toffee Bananas to be one of the best things on offer at our local Chinese restaurant, and was hugely pleased when I worked out how to cook them, so he could enjoy this at home too.

Beat the egg whites lightly in a bowl until frothy. Beat in the self-raising flour, 1 tablespoon at a time, to make a batter. Sprinkle a little plain flour over the bananas, then coat them in the batter.

Heat the oil in a wok or deep fryer to a temperature of 180°C (350°F), or until a cube of bread browns in 30 seconds. Fry the coated chunks of banana for about 5 minutes or until golden brown. Lift out with a slotted spoon and drain well on kitchen paper.

Have ready a bowl of cold water. Make the toffee. Combine the sugar and water in a saucepan; heat gently, stirring occasionally, until the sugar has dissolved. Add the butter, raise the heat and cook until the mixture forms a golden toffee. Quickly tip the drained bananas into the toffee, turning to coat them well, then, using a slotted spoon, dip them briefly in the cold water to harden the toffee. Drain and serve at once.

Serves 4

2 EGG WHITES

6 TABLESPOONS SELF-RAISING FLOUR

A LITTLE PLAIN FLOUR

4 BANANAS, QUARTERED

OIL, FOR DEEP-FRYING

TOFFEE

175 G (6 OZ) SUGAR

3 TABLESPOONS WATER

25 G (1 OZ) BUTTER

Party Pieces

The Great Down Under
Pavlova

If you don't mind, we won't enter the controversy about whether this famous confection comes from Australia or New Zealand, as I don't want to be lynched by either side. Let's all just agree that it is a wonderful light dessert named after a wonderful light ballerina, Anna Pavlova. It isn't quite the same as an ordinary meringue, as it should have a barely perceptible smooth creamy junction between the meringue and cream.

Line a large baking sheet with nonstick baking paper. Whisk the egg whites in a grease-free bowl until stiff, then gradually beat in the sugar, whisking until the mixture is very firm and glossy. Fold in the cornflour, vinegar and vanilla essence. Pile the meringue on to the lined baking sheet and spread it out with a spoon to make a large round or oval, at least 25 cm (10 inches) in diameter. Bake in a preheated oven, 120°C (250°F), Gas Mark ½, for 2-3 hours, until the meringue is crisp but not coloured. Allow to cool before peeling the meringue base carefully off the lining paper and placing it on a serving platter.

Shortly before serving, assemble the pavlova. Whip the cream until thick; spread it lightly over the top of the meringue. Scatter the strawberries on top. Scoop the passionfruit flesh out of the shells, spread over the strawberries and cream and serve.

Serves 8

4 EGG WHITES

250 G (8 OZ) CASTER SUGAR

1 TABLESPOON CORNFLOUR

2 TEASPOONS VINEGAR

1 TEASPOON VANILLA ESSENCE

TO FINISH

450 ML (¾ PINT) DOUBLE CREAM

500 G (1 LB) STRAWBERRIES, HULLED, HALVED IF LARGE

6 PASSIONFRUIT, HALVED

Left: *The Great Down Under Pavlova*

Zucotta

125 ML (4 FL OZ) CHERRY
BRANDY
200 G (7 OZ) SPONGE BISCUITS
200 G (7 OZ) PLAIN
CHOCOLATE, ROUGHLY
GRATED
450 ML (¾ PINT)
DOUBLE CREAM
125 ML (4 OZ) ICING SUGAR,
PLUS EXTRA FOR DUSTING
125 G (4 OZ) CHOPPED MIXED
NUTS, TOASTED AND COOLED

To make this rich and impressive Italian pudding, you will need a basin with a diameter of about 20 cm (8 inches) and a depth of 8 cm (3½ inches). Zucotta is the ideal choice for a large buffet, as it can be made well in advance. Provided it has been thoroughly chilled, it will retain its shape, even when left to stand for some time after unmoulding.

Line the pudding basin with clingfilm, leaving a generous overlap to cover the pudding. Put the cherry brandy in a shallow bowl. Dip each sponge finger in turn in the cherry brandy and line the base and sides of the bowl, keeping a few back to cover the top of the filling. The sponge fingers will be a little difficult to work with at first, as they remain rigid until the liqueur has soaked in, so put them roughly in place at this stage, and smooth the sponge lining with the back of a tablespoon before adding the filling.

Set 1 tablespoon of the grated chocolate aside for the decoration. Melt half the remaining chocolate in a small heatproof bowl over a saucepan of simmering water. Meanwhile, whip the cream and the icing sugar together in a bowl until soft peaks form; fold in the nuts and remaining grated chocolate to form a stiff mixture. Spoon half the filling carefully into the sponge-lined bowl, covering the base and sponge fingers, but leaving a hollow in the centre.

When the melted chocolate is smooth, cool it slightly by transferring it to another bowl, then stir in the remainder of the creamy nut mixture. The filling should be just enough to fill the hollow in the pudding. Arrange the reserved sponge fingers over the filling, keeping them as level as possible.

Fold the clingfilm over the pudding to cover it completely, put a plate on top and add a suitable small weight (less than 500 g/1 lb). Chill in the refrigerator for 3 hours or overnight.

When ready to serve, invert the zucotta on to a chilled serving plate, remove the wrapping, dust with icing sugar and the reserved grated chocolate.

Serves 10-12

Nanny's Lemon Fluff

You can make this light, wobbly dessert in long-stemmed glasses or small moulds. If using the latter, rinse them with cold water before adding the pudding mixture, and unmould carefully on to chilled plates before decorating.

Chill the evaporated milk in the refrigerator. Put the lemon juice in a heatproof bowl, sprinkle the gelatine on to the surface and set aside until spongy. Place the bowl over simmering water, stirring until the gelatine has dissolved, then remove from the heat and stir in the lemon rind. Set aside to infuse.

In a mixing bowl, whisk the egg yolks with half the sugar until pale and fluffy. Whisk the egg whites in a separate, grease-free bowl until stiff. Gradually whisk in the rest of the sugar until the mixture is smooth, firm and glossy. In another bowl, whisk the chilled evaporated milk until it triples in volume – a hand-held electric mixer is useful for this.

Strain the warm lemon juice mixture into the egg yolks and sugar, mix well, then quickly fold in the evaporated milk and beaten egg whites. Pour into glasses or rinsed moulds and leave to set in the refrigerator.

Meanwhile frost the rose petals. Dip them into the egg white, then into the caster sugar. Spread out to dry on kitchen paper. The petals may look more attractive if only the edges are frosted – very fine petals may become soggy if frosted all over.

Unmould the puddings if necessary. Decorate each with a flower shape made from frosted rose petals and an angelica 'stem'. Serve at once.

Serves 8

300 ML (½ PINT)
EVAPORATED MILK
GRATED RIND AND JUICE
OF 3 LEMONS
11 G (½ OZ) SACHET
POWDERED GELATINE
2 LARGE EGGS, SEPARATED
125 G (4 OZ) CASTER SUGAR
STRIPS OF ANGELICA
FROSTED ROSE PETALS
CLEAN UNBLEMISHED ROSE
PETALS
EGG WHITE, SLIGHTLY
BEATEN
CASTER SUGAR

Mille-Feuille

175 G (6 OZ) PUFF PASTRY,
THAWED IF FROZEN

6 KIWIFRUIT, PEELED

ICING SUGAR, FOR DREDGING

PASTRY CREAM

2 EGG YOLKS

50 G (2 OZ) CASTER SUGAR

I TABLESPOON CORNFLOUR

300 ML (½ PINT) MILK

150 ML (¼ PINT) DOUBLE
CREAM

A thousand leaves seems an awful lot, but there do appear to be dozens of layers in a good crisp flaky pastry. You can use any fruit in season for the filling, but I find that concentrating on a single variety which goes well with the custard cream is better than a mixture.

Cut the pastry in half and roll it out into 2 long rectangles of equal size, each less than 5 mm (¼ inch) thick. Put the rectangles on to a lightly greased baking sheet and prick them both all over with a fork. Bake in a preheated oven, 220°C (425°F), Gas Mark 7, for 10 minutes. Both pieces of pastry should be puffed and golden on the top; carefully turn them over and return to the oven for a further 3 minutes to brown and crisp the undersides. Cool on a wire rack. Split each rectangle of pastry in half lengthways; trim the sides straight to make 4 neat rectangles of equal size.

Make the pastry cream. Mix the egg yolks, sugar and cornflour to a smooth paste. In a pan, bring the milk to just below boiling point, then gradually stir the milk into the egg yolk mixture. Return the mixture to a clean pan and heat gently, stirring constantly until the custard thickens. As soon as it starts to thicken, remove from the heat and beat well to avoid lumps. Cover and cool.

Whip the cream until thick, then fold into the custard. Slice 2 of the kiwifruit for decoration; dice the rest.

Put 1 layer of pastry on a serving dish and spread a third of the pastry cream over it. Add a third of the diced fruit, spreading evenly over the custard, then put the next pastry layer on top. Repeat the layers until all the custard, fruit and pastry have been used, finishing with a layer of pastry. Dredge the top with icing sugar, and arrange the reserved kiwifruit slices in an overlapping line down the centre. Serve in slices.

Serves 6

Right: *Mille-Feuille*

Brazilian Mousse

125 G (4 OZ) PLAIN
CHOCOLATE, BROKEN INTO
SQUARES
3 TABLESPOONS RUM OR
ORANGE JUICE
125 G (4 OZ) CASTER SUGAR
5 EGGS, SEPARATED
125 G (4 OZ) BRAZIL NUTS
300 ML (½ PINT)
DOUBLE CREAM
TO DECORATE
WHIPPED CREAM
CRYSTALLIZED VIOLETS

Brazil nuts are gathered from huge trees in the Amazonian rainforest, and because they are one obvious crop from which money can be made, I was encouraged when in Brazil to come up with lots of recipes for these delicious nuts – to help save the rainforest. A small contribution to a major problem, perhaps, but you might like to feel, as this delicious concoction melts in your mouth, that it isn't as wicked as it seems.

Melt the chocolate with the rum or orange juice in a large heatproof bowl over a saucepan of barely simmering water. When most of the chocolate has melted, add the sugar. Stir until it has melted into the chocolate to make a smooth sauce. Take the bowl off the heat and cool slightly.

Beat the egg yolks, one at a time, into the chocolate mixture. Finely grind the shelled nuts, preferably in a food processor, and stir them into the chocolate mixture. In another bowl, whip the cream until it holds its shape. Whisk the egg whites in a separate, grease-free bowl until stiff. Fold the cream into the chocolate and nut mixture, then lightly fold in the beaten egg whites. Pour the mixture into individual glass dishes and chill in the refrigerator for several hours before serving.

Decorate each pudding with a whirl of whipped cream and some crystallized violet petals.

Serves 8

Triple Chocolate Eggs

Easter wouldn't be Easter without lots of luscious chocolates. If you have been given more eggs than even a chocoholic can manage, you might like to try using up the half shells in this recipe. Smaller eggs – about 7 cm (3 inches) in length – are best, as this is a very rich dessert. If eggs of a suitable size are not available, use chocolate shells or cups.

If you buy the chocolate eggs, they will probably be stuck together. The easiest way to separate them into halves is to cut along the join with a sawing action, using a narrow-bladed serrated knife.

Put the egg halves, shells or cups on to a large serving platter, propping them up with crumpled yellow tissue paper if necessary.

Make the filling. Melt the white chocolate in a heatproof bowl over a saucepan of barely simmering water. Off the heat, stir in the soured cream or crème fraîche, with the Bailey's or rum. Stir until smooth. In a separate bowl, whip the double cream until soft peaks form; fold into the chocolate mixture.

Fill the egg halves, cups or shells with the white chocolate filling. Put them in the refrigerator or a cool place for several hours or overnight to set. The filling does not set hard, but has a dense mousse-like consistency. When set, sprinkle a little of the grated chocolate or crumbled Flake over each filled egg, shell or cup and serve.

Makes 16

8 x 7 cm (3 inch) hollow chocolate eggs or 16 chocolate shells or cups
grated plain chocolate or crumbled chocolate flake, to decorate
FILLING
250 g (8 oz) white chocolate, broken into squares
300 ml (½ pint) soured cream or crème fraîche
2 tablespoons Bailey's irish cream liqueur or rum
300 ml (½ pint) double cream

Croquembouche

CHOUX PASTRY

4 EGGS

300 ML (½ PINT) WATER

125 G (4 OZ) BUTTER

150 G (5 OZ) STRONG PLAIN

FLOUR

4 TEASPOONS SUGAR

FILLING

600 ML (1 PINT) DOUBLE

CREAM

1 TABLESPOON INSTANT

COFFEE GRANULES

3 TABLESPOONS TIA MARIA OR

OTHER COFFEE-FLAVOURED

LIQUEUR

SUGAR GLAZE

150 G (5 OZ) GRANULATED

SUGAR

150 ML (¼ PINT) WATER

The word means crunch-in-the-mouth and refers to the crackle from the glazed sugar coating on a pyramid of delectable cream puffs. Don't be anxious about boiling the sugar, simply take care and have handy a bowl of cold water in which to stand the saucepan if the syrup seems to be in danger of overheating; this will arrest further cooking.

Make the choux pastry following the instructions for Profiteroles (see page 100), baking the puffs in several batches. Cool on wire racks.

Whip the cream for the filling in a bowl until thick. Dissolve the coffee in the minimum amount of boiling water in a cup, then add this, with the liqueur, to the cream. Whip again until the mixture is thick enough to pipe. Fill the puffs as when making the profiteroles.

To make the sugar glaze, combine the sugar and the measured water in a heavy-bottomed saucepan. Heat gently, stirring slowly until all the sugar has dissolved. Bring to the boil without any further stirring and cook until the syrup registers 140°C (275°F) on a sugar thermometer. Alternatively, test by dropping a teaspoon of the syrup into a cup of cold water; if it forms a thread which snaps rather than bends when you try to break it, the syrup is ready.

Remove the pan from the heat. Using tongs or a skewer, carefully dip the cream-filled puffs in the hot syrup, immersing them no more than halfway. Arrange a ring of puffs on a decorative serving platter, sticking them together with the syrup, then build up a cone shape with the remaining puffs. Any remaining syrup may be drizzled down the finished cone, and should cool to a cracking consistency.

Serves 12

Right: *Croquembouche*

Cononley Cream

125 G (4 OZ) FRESH BROWN
BREADCRUMBS
125 G (4 OZ) DEMERARA
SUGAR
5 TEASPOONS INSTANT COFFEE
GRANULES
4 TABLESPOONS DRINKING
CHOCOLATE POWDER
600 ML (1 PINT) WHIPPING
CREAM

I was given this recipe by my friend Shirley, who has an even bigger family than mine. They all descend upon her at holiday time and if she has a day's notice, she often makes this quick and easy pudding.

Mix the breadcrumbs, sugar, coffee and chocolate in a bowl. Whip the cream until it starts to hold its shape. Put a layer of dry mixture in a glass bowl. Cover with a thin layer of cream. Sprinkle 2 tablespoons of the dry mixture over the cream; continue adding alternate layers of cream and crumbs, finishing with a thin sprinkling of crumbs. Chill for several hours or overnight before serving.
Serves 8

Chestnut Parfait

50 G (2 OZ) GLACÉ CHERRIES
50 G (2 OZ) SULTANAS
50 G (2 OZ) MIXED PEEL
50 G (2 OZ) RAISINS
6 TABLESPOONS RUM OR
BRANDY
4 EGG YOLKS
250 G (8 OZ) ICING SUGAR
600 ML (1 PINT) DOUBLE
CREAM
125 G (4 OZ) CANNED
CHESTNUT PURÉE
TO DECORATE
WHIPPED CREAM
PIECES OF MARRONS GLACÉS

Put the cherries, sultanas, peel and raisins in a bowl. Stir in the rum or brandy. Cover and soak for several hours or overnight, stirring occasionally until the fruit has swelled and absorbed the alcohol.

Whisk the egg yolks and sugar until pale and frothy. Heat three-quarters of the cream over simmering water, then gradually whisk into the yolks and sugar. Return the mixture to the bowl, replace over hot water and stir until it thickens sufficiently to coat the back of a wooden spoon. Remove from the heat. Put the chestnut purée in a bowl, add a little custard and beat until smooth. Add a little more custard, beat, then add the chestnut mixture to remaining custard; mix. Cover and freeze for 2-3 hours until thick and slushy. Line a pudding basin with clingfilm. Whip remaining cream until thick. Fold into chestnut mixture with the fruits and alcohol. Put into the basin and freeze. An hour before serving, remove and stand for 30 minutes. Turn out and decorate with cream and marrons glacés. Stand for 30 minutes more. Serve
Serves 10

Piggy Pudding

A memorable television encounter with Miss Piggy resulted in this luscious dessert fit for a star — and what a big star she is!

Mark 4 x 23 cm (9 inch) circles on separate pieces of nonstick baking paper and place the paper on baking sheets. Whisk the egg whites in a grease-free bowl until firm peaks form, then gradually whisk in the sugar until stiff and glossy. Set aside one-quarter of the flaked almonds for the topping. Chop the rest finely, either by hand or in a food processor; fold the nuts into the meringue mixture.

Spread the meringue on the marked circles to make rounds of equal thickness. Bake in a preheated oven, 150°C (300°F), Gas Mark 2, for 2-2½ hours or until just crisp. Cool before peeling off the baking paper.

Put the chocolate in a heatproof bowl. Bring half the cream to just below boiling point in a saucepan. Pour the hot cream over the chocolate, stirring all the time, until the chocolate melts to form a smooth sauce (ganache). Cool, then chill, stirring or whisking the ganache occasionally as it thickens.

Just before serving, whip the remaining cream in a bowl until it holds its shape. Sandwich the meringue layers with the whipped cream, peach halves and chocolate ganache. Sprinkle the reserved flaked almonds over the top.

Serves 10

6 LARGE EGG WHITES

375 G (12 OZ) CASTER SUGAR

200 G (7 OZ) FLAKED ALMONDS

300 G (10 OZ) PLAIN CHOCOLATE, BROKEN INTO SQUARES

600 ML (1 PINT) DOUBLE CREAM

2 X 410 G (13½ OZ) CANS PEACH HALVES, DRAINED

Hadrian's Wall

This pudding will happily sit on a buffet table, and because you can make it well in advance – the day before if necessary – it is a good choice when entertaining a large number of guests.

2 x 200 G (7 OZ) PACKETS
SPONGE FINGERS
300 ML (½ PINT) SHERRY
600 ML (1 PINT) DOUBLE
CREAM
2 TABLESPOONS INSTANT
COFFEE GRANULES
3 TABLESPOONS ICING SUGAR

You will need a fairly long, narrow serving dish for this, as the construction is like that of a brick wall! Have the biscuits ready to hand, and pour the sherry into a shallow bowl ready for dipping.

Whip the cream in a large bowl until it starts to thicken. In a cup, dissolve the coffee in the minimum amount of boiling water; pour this on to the cream with the icing sugar. Whip until the cream is thick again and is the colour of pale coffee. It should be thick enough to hold its shape, as this is the 'cement' for the wall. The 'bricks' are the sponge fingers, which should be dipped for only a moment in the sherry before being placed side by side on the serving dish to form a bottom layer. Try to use about a quarter of the biscuits in this first layer, depending on the size of your serving dish.

Spread a layer of cream over the moistened fingers, then add the second layer of dipped sponge fingers, placing them at right angles to the first and cutting or trimming them as necessary. Continue building up the wall in this fashion, setting each successive layer of sponge fingers at right angles to the last, until all the ingredients have been used, finishing with a smooth layer of the coffee-flavoured cream. Chill until ready to serve.

Serves 12

Vacherin

This is a classic meringue dessert, flavoured with nuts – in this case, two sorts,
which makes it doubly delicious. You can usually buy chestnut purée around
Christmas time, when it is stocked in the shops for turkey stuffing.
If the chestnut purée is sweetened, leave out the icing sugar.

Mark 4 x 23 cm (9 inch) circles on separate pieces of nonstick baking paper and place the paper on baking sheets. Whisk the egg whites in a grease-free bowl until firm peaks form, then gradually whisk in the sugar until stiff and glossy. Grind the chopped toasted hazelnuts finely in a food processor; fold these into the meringue mixture.

Spread the meringue on the marked circles to make rounds of equal thickness. Bake in a preheated oven, 120°C (250°F), Gas Mark ½, for 2-3 hours or until crisp throughout. Cool before peeling off the baking paper.

No more than 1 hour before serving, assemble the dessert. Beat all the filling ingredients together in a bowl to make a thick smooth purée. Sandwich the meringue layers together with this mixture, finishing with a layer of meringue. To decorate, beat the double cream until thick, spoon it over the top of the vacherin and sprinkle with the chopped toasted hazelnuts. Dust lightly with cocoa powder. To serve, cut into wedges.

Serves 10-12

MERINGUE

6 EGG WHITES

375 G (12 OZ) CASTER SUGAR

150 G (5 OZ) HAZELNUTS,

TOASTED AND CHOPPED

FILLING

440 G (15 OZ) CAN

CHESTNUT PURÉE

125 G (4 OZ) ICING SUGAR

4 TABLESPOONS RUM

300 ML (½ PINT) DOUBLE

CREAM

TO DECORATE

150 ML (¼ PINT) DOUBLE

CREAM

50 G (2 OZ) HAZELNUTS,

TOASTED AND CHOPPED

COCOA POWDER, FOR DUSTING

Port Wine Jelly

600 ML (1 PINT) WATER

175 G (6 OZ) SUGAR

1 STICK CINNAMON

3 WHOLE CLOVES

GRATED RIND OF 1 ORANGE

3 X 11 G (½ OZ) SACHETS

POWDERED GELATINE

600 ML (1 PINT) PORT

8 SMALL BUNCHES OF

FROSTED REDCURRANTS, TO

DECORATE

We are always given a bottle or two of port around Christmas time, and we don't always drink it, so I've developed this easy pudding to use up some of the surplus. It makes a nice light finish to a rich winter feast.

Put 450 ml (¾ pint) of the measured water in a large saucepan with the sugar, cinnamon, cloves and grated orange rind. Bring to the boil, then remove the pan from the heat and set aside for 10 minutes to allow the flavours to infuse. Meanwhile, sprinkle the gelatine on to the remaining water in a small heat-proof bowl. Set aside until spongy, then stir into the hot spiced syrup until all the gelatine has dissolved. Strain the mixture into a large jug, add the port and stir well. Cool, then divide the mixture between 8 stemmed wine glasses; chill in the refrigerator or a cool place for several hours until set.

Frost the redcurrants, in the same way as for frosted rose petals (see page 145). When dry, place a bunch of frosted redcurrants on the rim of each glass. Serve at once.

Serves 8

Cooper's Cream

3 CRUNCHIE BARS

3 CHOCOLATE FLAKES

8 SMALL OR 4 LARGE

MERINGUE NESTS OR HALVES,

CHOPPED INTO 1 CM (½ INCH)

PIECES

600 ML (1 PINT) DOUBLE

CREAM

1 TEASPOON VANILLA ESSENCE

Cut the Crunchie bars and Flakes into chunks and then mix the meringue and chocolate pieces together in a large bowl. In another bowl, whip the cream with the vanilla essence until thick. Fold in the chocolate and meringue pieces, then pile the mixture into dishes and chill until set.

Alternatively, spoon the mixture into a ring mould and freeze for several hours. Unmould by dipping briefly into hot water and turning the pudding out on to a serving dish. The centre of the ring may be filled with a selection of chopped fresh fruits.

Serves 8-10

Orange Charlotte Russe

This dessert is not expensive, yet looks impressive, so is well worth spending some time on. It makes a striking centrepiece for a buffet table, especially if you tie a green ribbon around it.

Line an 18 cm (7 inch) round soufflé dish with clingfilm, leaving an overlap to cover the pudding. Pour the juice from the can of mandarins into a measuring jug and make up to 500 ml (17 fl oz) with boiling water. Pour over the jelly in a bowl and stir until melted. Spoon 2-3 tablespoons of the jelly on to the base of dish. Dip the sponge fingers briefly into the remaining jelly and line the dish by standing the fingers next to each other around the sides – they may stick up slightly above the rim. Reserve the remaining sponge fingers.

Arrange some of the mandarins in a neat pattern over the jelly in the dish, spoon 2-3 tablespoons more jelly over the oranges and put the dish in the refrigerator so that the jelly sets. Place half of the remaining orange jelly in a bowl and place it in the refrigerator to set too. This will take at least 30 minutes. Keep the rest of the jelly in a warm place so that it remains liquid.

When the bowl of jelly is almost set, whip the cream until thick in a separate bowl; stir in the jelly and pour this carefully into the centre of the dish, over the jellied oranges, and chill for 30 minutes more.

When the creamy mixture seems set, arrange the remaining mandarins on top, then fill the space in the centre of the dish with the remaining sponge fingers, dipping them in the remaining liquid jelly. Trim the tops of the edging fingers level with the top of the filling, then pour any remaining liquid jelly over the top. Fold the edges of the clingfilm over to cover, and put a plate and small weight on top to compress it. Chill for several hours or overnight, until set.

To serve, fold the clingfilm back, invert a serving plate over the dish, then, holding them firmly together, turn both upside down and remove, using the edges of the clingfilm to ease to pudding out.

Serves 8-10

397 G (14 OZ) CAN
MANDARIN ORANGES
142 G (5 OZ) TABLET ORANGE
JELLY, BROKEN
INTO CUBES
200 G (7 OZ) SPONGE FINGERS
200 ML (7 FL OZ) DOUBLE
CREAM

Index